The Essential Guide To Parenting Boys With ADHD

Empowering Parents with Scientific Strategies for Behavior Management, Academic Success, and Social Well-Being

Copyright R J Carroll © 2024 All rights reserved

The content contained within this book may not be reproduced, duplicated or transmitted without direct written permission from the author or the publisher.

Under no circumstances will any blame or legal responsibility be held against the publisher, or author, for any damages, reparation, or monetary loss due to the information contained within this book. Either directly or indirectly. You are responsible for your own choices, actions, and results.

Legal Notice:

This book is copyright protected. This book is only for personal use. You cannot amend, distribute, sell, use, quote or paraphrase any part, or the content within this book, without the consent of the author or publisher.

Disclaimer Notice:

Please note the information contained within this document is for educational and entertainment purposes only. All effort has been executed to present accurate, up to date, and reliable, complete information. No warranties of any kind are declared or implied. Readers acknowledge that the author is not engaging in the rendering of legal, financial, medical or professional advice. The content within this book has been derived from various sources. Please consult a licensed professional before attempting any techniques outlined in this book.

By reading this document, the reader agrees that under no circumstances is the author responsible for any losses, direct or indirect, which are incurred as a result of the use of the information contained within this document, including, but not limited to, — errors, omissions, or inaccuracies.

About the Author

R.J. Carroll is a dedicated child and adolescent psychotherapist specializing in ADHD and a devoted mother to a son with ADHD. Combining years of clinical expertise with personal experience, she is deeply passionate about providing parents with the tools and insights needed to support their neurodivergent children. With compassion and practical advice, she aims to help families navigate the rewarding and challenging journey of raising neurodivergent children.

This book is dedicated to my son, Max, whose journey fuels my passion.

Table of Contents

Introduction 7
   What Is ADHD? 9
   Executive Functioning and ADHD 10
   The Purpose of This Book 11

Chapter 1: The 4-1-1 on ADHD in Boys 13
   Understanding the Different Types of ADHD in Boys 15
   Shifting Your Perspective: ADHD as a Neurodiversity, NOT a Disorder 17
   Understanding Treatment Options 22
   Chapter Takeaways 27

Chapter 2: Building a Supportive Home for Your Son 28
   Creating a Supportive Home Environment 29
   Foolproof Way of Collaborating with Schools 33
   Filling Your Social Calendar with Like-Minded Parents ... 34
   Chapter Takeaways 36

Chapter 3: Uncovering and Addressing Sensory Triggers ... 38
   Sensory Overload: The Common Sensory Triggers 40
   Teaching Your Son to Recognize His Sensory Triggers 42
   Chapter Takeaways 55

Chapter 4: Navigating the Storm of Your Son's Intense Emotions 56
   Embracing Your Son's Emotional Intelligence 59
   Teaching Your Son Coping Skills 60
   Addressing Comorbid Conditions 64
   Chapter Takeaways 67

Chapter 5: Boosting Your Son's Executive Function & Problem-Solving Skills 69
   Developing Your Son's Planning & Organizational Skills ... 71
   Strengthening His Focus, Attention, and Working Memory ... 73
   Teaching Your Son How to Problem-Solve 75
   Parenting in a Way That Encourages Independence 78
   Embracing Your Son's Mistakes, and Teaching Him to Do the Same 80
   Chapter Takeaways 82

Chapter 6: Setting Your Son Up for Life with Healthy Habits 83
The Power of the Almighty Sleep Schedule 84
Nutrition and Exercise: The Healthy Habit Essentials...................... 88
Say "No" to Endless Screen Time 89
Chapter Takeaways 92

Chapter 7: Helping Your Son Build Positive Relationships 94
Strengthening Your Bond with Your Son 95
Helping Your Son Through Peer Relationships................................ 98
Sibling Stresses: How to Help Siblings Understand...................... 100
Chapter Takeaways 103

Chapter 8: Showing Your Son His Superpowers & Developing His Interests 105
Your Son's Superpowers: Seeing His ADHD Differently 106
Strategies for You to Stay Energized and Effective 109
Chapter Takeaways 112

Chapter 9: Planning for Changes & Transitions...............................113
Transitioning to New Environments.. 114
Preparing for Adolescence 118
Transitioning into Adulthood 120
Chapter Takeaways 122

Chapter 10: Mastering the Art of Self-Care When You Have a Son with ADHD...123
How Caring for Yourself Makes You a Better Parent..................... 124
Chapter Takeaways 127

Wrapping It Up 128

References 131

Introduction

> *"Why fit in when you were born to stand out?"*
> – Dr. Seuss

Roughly six million children ages 3-17 had an ADHD diagnosis between 2016-2019 (Centers for Disease Control and Prevention, 2023). So, if you're right in the middle of parenting a boy with ADHD, you're not alone. Did you ever think you'd be in this situation, struggling to understand your son and managing his emotions and behaviors? My guess is, you didn't. That's certainly how it was for me.

I was once in your shoes. As a family therapist specializing in ADHD, I had plenty of professional experience working with people parenting a child with ADHD. Yet I always felt distanced from ADHD—it was a part of my working world, not my home life. After all, I don't personally have ADHD, and neither does anyone else in my family. So, it's safe to say that I thought my child would never struggle with ADHD. Haha. How wrong was I?

The phone calls home began when Max was in preschool. He got a telling-off during circle time for talking out of turn. During bathroom breaks, he was told off again for spending too long over the sink, singing the song he'd learned during music time that day, and seemingly not paying any attention to his teacher's instructions. This wasn't the last of it—far from it, in fact. He was often scolded for standing up at his seat, touching posters on the walls when he was supposed to be standing in single file, and talking when the teacher was talking. At the end of his last year of preschool—after a year of tellings-off, phone calls home, and signs of distractedness creeping into our home life—an assessment revealed that he scored in the 99th percentile for ADHD.

My son's struggles at preschool prompted me to finally schedule an appointment with his pediatrician. I was hesitant though, which is funny to say, since I was a family therapist. You would have thought I'd follow the steps I outline for families, taking my own advice and doing everything by the book. Yet something stopped me—maybe I knew life was going to get more complicated. Perhaps I was in denial. Or maybe, just maybe, no matter how much I knew otherwise, it still felt like I had done something wrong and failed Max in some way. I want to be super clear here: I have never considered ADHD a bad thing. We're all different in our own way, and some of us need support for those differences. Yet when you're facing an ADHD diagnosis for your child, you can't help but feel like you've done something wrong or like life's going to get a lot harder from here, right?

Anyway, back to the pediatrician. I shared the school's assessment results with the pediatrician and told him about the signs I'd seen at home. After talking with me about Max's symptoms and reviewing a parent checklist I had completed, the pediatrician diagnosed Max with ADHD, combined presentation. So began the journey of parenting a neurodivergent child.

I consider Max and myself to be pretty lucky, really. He got his ADHD diagnosis when he was only four years old. For many, I know the road isn't so straightforward. There can be years of phone calls home, reports describing your child in all the negative ways under the sun, and teachers thinking your child doesn't want to learn or is just plain defiant.

I totally get it. I understand how unequipped you can feel as a parent with a child with an ADHD diagnosis. I mean, I was a trained professional in ADHD, for goodness' sake! And I still wasn't mentally or emotionally prepared. To be really, truly prepared, you need to not only learn a lot about ADHD but also find out all the best ways to support a young boy with an ADHD diagnosis. You know what else? You need to know that people are right alongside you, fighting the fight for their sons, too— you're not alone.

This book will give you support. It's a messy journey, and I won't sugarcoat it, but I will help you feel prepared and give you the tools to support your son, so he has the best shot in this chaotic, pressured, and often unfair world for a kid with ADHD.

What Is ADHD?

Before getting ahead of myself and diving into the specifics of parenting a boy with ADHD, let's start with the fundamentals. What is ADHD? Sometimes, people believe that children with ADHD simply have a hard time paying attention or that they just can't sit still. In some instances (the worst kind), people may even believe that ADHD is just a symptom of bad parenting or a sign that a child is poorly behaved. I want to lay this out clear as day: ADHD has nothing to do with poor parenting, and it is far more complex than having a hard time sitting still or paying attention.

First, it's helpful to understand the diagnostic criteria for ADHD. Perhaps you already know these criteria; you may have been given a speedy run-through by your pediatrician and sent home with a little leaflet. If you're anything like me in those first few stages of your son's ADHD diagnosis, you didn't take a whole lot in. So, let's go over it. To diagnose ADHD, clinicians use the *Diagnostic and Statistical Manual of Mental Disorders*, which is currently in its fifth edition. According to this manual, ADHD is a neurodevelopmental disorder, meaning symptoms of the condition typically appear early in life, often before a child begins school (supposedly, but after speaking with many parents, I know how many kids slip under the radar). To be diagnosed with ADHD, a child must have a persistent pattern of symptoms that interferes with their life in a significant way (American Psychiatric Association, 2022). So, if you need the proof, here is it: ADHD is much more than simply having a hard time paying attention.

A child with ADHD can be diagnosed as having predominantly inattentive type, predominantly hyperactive/impulsive type, or a combined presentation, with symptoms of both inattention and hyperactivity/impulsivity present. A child must show six symptoms of inattention, hyperactivity/impulsivity, or both to be diagnosed. Symptoms of inattention include being unable to pay attention to details or remain on-task, and also difficulty completing schoolwork and chores, being organized, and staying focused on tasks that require them to exert brain power. Symptoms of hyperactivity/impulsivity include difficulty waiting for their turn, as well as behaviors like fidgeting, climbing or running when it's not appropriate to do so, interrupting others, and talking "excessively" (American Psychiatric Association, 2023).

So, the diagnostic criteria and symptoms of ADHD speak for themselves; this is a complex condition we have here. Boys who have ADHD struggle to pay attention and regulate their behaviors to the extent that it can interfere with their schoolwork and social relationships. ADHD symptoms don't just show up then go away—they're continuous. If your son struggles through homework assignments, or interrupts and talks over you all the time, as my son does, you'll know what I mean.

The bottom line is that ADHD is so much more than sometimes having a hard time paying attention. All of us can struggle with concentration from time to time, and you hear people throwing around phrases like, "I'm a bit ADHD" all the time. But for a boy with ADHD, the symptoms are so persistent that it's difficult for them to do their best or even just get by in the normal school environment.

Executive Functioning and ADHD

If you're new to executive functioning, here's a quick whistle-stop tour: executive function is a set of skills that our brain has. The executive skill set includes working memory, a skill that helps us keep information in mind while we're working on a task. Basically, it helps us remember information we need for a task, during a task. Flexible thinking and self-control are also key elements of our executive functions; these skills help us to think about things in a new way and control our impulses, respectively.

Experts call executive function the "management system of the brain" because it helps us to plan, set goals, and get tasks done (Goldstein & Naglieri, 2014). When we struggle with these skills, then, it not only impacts our life at home, but also at school or work, and in life in general. And, you guessed it, this is believed by many to be one of the key areas of difficulty for kids with ADHD. Slight caveat here though: there is some debate on this, with some experts still believing that ADHD doesn't include executive function skills.

Yet, more and more research suggests a link between ADHD and executive function. Take a study from 2018 by Kofler and colleagues. They found that 89% of children with ADHD had an impairment in at least one executive functioning area. This is an important statistic, as executive functions are not only involved in planning life decisions and goals, but also in the regulation, planning, and control of behavior. As such, difficulties with executive functioning may explain many of the struggles that children with ADHD face with their behaviors (Pineda-Alhucema et al., 2018).

Understanding the relationship between executive functions and ADHD can be a powerful tool for us parents for two reasons. First, the fact that these difficulties are linked to ADHD shows that ADHD involves much more than simply being squirmy, disruptive, or unfocused (terms I've heard used by Max's teachers on more than a handful of occasions). Second, the fortunate reality is that boys with ADHD, like Max and your son, can use their strengths to help them overcome these difficulties with executive function. Yet, we can't help our sons if we don't have all of the information at our disposal, and the tools to change this knowledge into effective strategies.

That's what this book is all about: helping you support your son so he can harness his strengths in order to overcome the challenges that come with ADHD.

The Purpose of This Book

Knowledge is power, but it isn't enough to simply learn about ADHD, as this won't give you the practical tools you need to support your child. So, this book presents a unique combination: it's jam-packed full of information about ADHD so you can become an expert ADHD parent, and strategies that will be invaluable for both you *and* your son.

After reading this book, this is where you'll be:

- You'll understand the superpowers that boys with ADHD possess.

- You'll learn how to leverage your son's strengths to help him overcome the challenges that come with ADHD.
- You'll build your son's toolkit of self-soothing techniques so he can cope with triggers and intense emotions in healthy ways (without behavioral outbursts).
- You'll arm yourself with routines and behavioral management plans that actually *work* for your son.
- You'll support your son in developing social skills, and empathy for you, the rest of the family, and the wider world.

I'll guide you along the way, as we work toward getting you to a point where you feel confident in every outcome listed above. I bring with me not only firsthand experience of raising a son with ADHD, but experience treating children with ADHD as a practicing clinician. I've seen both sides of the story: the deeply personal side and the practical side. As a bonus, I've spent tons of time researching best practices for ADHD treatment and not only supporting my son to learn these practices, but also teaching them to the next generation of clinicians.

So, without further ado, are you ready to begin your journey to becoming a parent who's equipped with everything ADHD has to throw at you? Join me in Chapter 1, where you'll learn how to use your son's restlessness and energy as a strength.

Chapter 1: The 4-1-1 on ADHD in Boys

"Strength lies in differences, not in similarities."
– Stephen R. Covey

When we consider who first described ADHD, the answers are mixed. Some say that the first clinical description of ADHD as we know it now, with the same symptoms, came from British pediatrician George F. Still in 1902. Yet, some attribute the origin of ADHD to another, Sir Alexander Crichton, a Scottish doctor who reported the set of symptoms attributed to ADHD way back in 1798.

Despite the difference of opinion in who first set their cap at ADHD, the term "ADHD" in its current form wasn't recognized widely recognized until 1980, when it was published in the *Diagnostic and Statistical Manual of Mental Disorders*, the handbook used by US healthcare professionals to diagnose mental disorders. Before this point, it was known by many different names, including:

- Organic drivenness
- Minimal brain dysfunction
- Hyperkinesis
- Hyperactive syndrome
- Attention deficit disorder

Now, why am I telling you this? Well, it's important to recognize that understanding ADHD is as straightforward as getting an ADHD diagnosis—in other words, not at all straightforward! There is a lot that isn't known about ADHD, so if you're confused by the information out there, or you seem to be getting conflicting information from different people, this is likely why.

As parents of kids with ADHD, we have to throw out what we thought we knew about ADHD and embrace new information. For example, when I first found out about ADHD, I thought that both boys and girls could have ADHD, and they usually did in equal measures. It wasn't until later on that I found out ADHD doesn't affect boys and girls equally—it's far more commonly diagnosed in boys. In fact, 13% of boys are diagnosed with ADHD compared to 6% of girls (Centers for Disease Control and Prevention, 2022). However, research shows that this seems to level out in adulthood, which could suggest that ADHD may just be misdiagnosed in girls compared to boys due to the difference in symptoms.

What are these differing symptoms? Let's take a look.

ADHD Symptoms in Boys	**ADHD Symptoms in Girls**
<ul><li>Talking non-stop</li><li>Struggling to sit or stand still</li><li>Impulsivity</li><li>Interrupting conversations, activities, etc.</li><li>Overactive (and sometimes aggressive) behavior</li></ul>	<ul><li>Anxiety</li><li>Difficulty listening</li><li>Inattentiveness</li><li>Low self-esteem</li><li>Requiring extra support with homework</li><li>Executive functioning difficulties</li><li>Underachieving in school</li></ul>

(Drake Institute of Neurphysical Medicine, n.d.).

But let's get one thing straight—not all boys with ADHD present with the same challenges. There are three types of ADHD in boys, and each of them is slightly different from the other.

Understanding the Different Types of ADHD in Boys

We have a saying at my workplace: Once you've met one person with ADHD, you've met one person with ADHD. Basically, what we mean by it is this: every ADHD presentation is unique. Some people are more hyperactive, while others struggle mostly with being unfocused and distracted. So, it's important that, as parents of boys with ADHD, we get to know our son's uniqueness rather than focusing word-for-word on the ADHD symptoms we read about.

What's more, it's easy to assume when you first hear about ADHD, that it is just that, ADHD and that there is only one type. In fact, there are three primary types of ADHD: inattentive type, hyperactive-impulsive type, and combined type—each with a different pattern of behaviors (Substance Abuse and Mental Health Services Administration, 2016).

INATTENTIVE TYPE ADHD

As the name suggests, children diagnosed with inattentive type ADHD experience symptoms of inattention more often than impulsivity and hyperactivity. This doesn't mean that they won't struggle with hyperactivity or controlling their impulses; it just means that these aren't the most prevalent characteristics of inattentive ADHD.

Children with inattentive type ADHD tend to struggle most with tasks involving planning and organization (Langberg & Epstein, 2009). For example, they might always be losing their belongings, lose focus quickly, and forget to do important tasks like their homework, rushing through it at the last minute or handing it in while still incomplete.

You may also catch them daydreaming a lot of the time, as this is a common trait of children with inattentive type ADHD, and this may mean they look like they're not listening. They also tend to struggle with boredom, procrastination, and following directions.

HYPERACTIVE-IMPULSIVE TYPE ADHD

Children with hyperactive-impulsive type ADHD are often extremely hyperactive and impulsive, typically showing more signs of these characteristics than inattention.

If your son is a hyperactive-impulsive type, you've likely noticed him fidgeting most of the time, either by tapping his hands or feet, jiggling his leg, or squirming in his seat. Children with this form of ADHD often find sitting still physically uncomfortable, so they tend to get up out of their seats, leaving the classroom or dinner table unexpectedly.

Boys with hyperactive-impulsive ADHD also typically climb and run at any opportunity, and there may be a running joke (get the pun?) that your son is always on the move. When he plays, he likely plays LOUDLY, and he may talk excessively without pausing for breath. Hyperactive-impulsive type ADHD is also characterized by difficulty holding onto thoughts and waiting for one's turn, so your son may blurt out his thoughts, interrupting you and others and butting into conversations. This may get your son in particular trouble at school, especially if he says the answer out loud instead of putting his hand up.

COMBINATION TYPE ADHD

Combination type ADHD is the most common subtype of ADHD (Johns Hopkins Medicine, n.d.). Children with combined type ADHD (like my son Max) don't swing one way more than the other—they don't predominantly show hyperactivity, impulsivity, *or* inattention, but rather a combination of all of these.

So, if your son has combined type ADHD, he may struggle to concentrate in class, and find it hard to stay in his seat for family meals or really for any activity that requires stillness. He may also show any and all of the symptoms listed in the previous two ADHD subtypes.

Of all the difficulties, though, children with combined type ADHD tend to find behavioral inhibition the most challenging. This means that they'll often interrupt you while you're talking, blurt things out as soon as they come to mind, get out of their seat at inconvenient times like during lessons or at dinner, and play loudly.

Unfortunately, it isn't just boys' behaviors that are impacted by their ADHD diagnosis. If this were the case, it might be easier to support them and manage. Instead, it's the impact that these behaviors have on their learning and interactions with other people that can cause the most problems.

Common ADHD characteristics tend to get painted incredibly badly in schools. You've likely experienced this with your son, like I have with Max. They're labeled as "defiant" and always told off for not paying attention. At one point, right before Max's ADHD assessment, his class teacher rang home and told me she'd kept count of the number of times she'd had to redirect him over the space of an hour—it averaged out at once every seven seconds.

What's maybe more upsetting to see than anything else is the way their classmates start to interact with them. Their impulsivity and behaviors associated with ADHD may make it difficult to form healthy, meaningful relationships with friends. According to recent stats, more than half of children with ADHD struggle with peer relationships (Mikami, 2021).

When you're dealing with this onslaught of negativity, you may catch yourself feeling these negative things about your son, too. I know I did when Max's school behavior was at its worst. However, by switching your mindset around his ADHD traits, you can not only begin to understand and support your son better, but you can also encourage his teachers to switch their mindsets and adapt, and improve your son's self-esteem, too.

Shifting Your Perspective: ADHD as a Neurodiversity, NOT a Disorder

In the early research on ADHD, experts talked about it in all kinds of negative ways—referring to it as a "deficit" or a "disability", and often suggesting that those with ADHD are lacking in some way. Even now, we still call it attention deficit hyperactivity *disorder*. If the words "deficit" and "disorder" don't scream negativity, I don't know what does.

As parents of sons with ADHD, we can get into a rut of negativity, a perspective known as the deficit-based model. The Oxford definition of the deficit model is:

> "A perspective which attributes failures such as lack of achievement, learning, or success in gaining employment to a personal lack of effort or deficiency in the individual, rather than to failures or limitations of the education and training system or to prevalent socio-economic trends."

So, in other words, kids with ADHD get labeled as deficient in some way due to their struggles within the learning environment, and in societal environments as a whole. Yet, let's consider for a second—is it really a deficiency? The answer is no, it's not. There's no denying that children with ADHD differ from other children—we do them a disservice if we don't recognize this. Yet there is a key distinction between *differences* and *deficits*.

When we label our children as having a deficiency or disorder, we do three things:

1. We automatically limit their capabilities

This perspective leads us to have lower expectations of our children. Without even knowing it, we can begin to limit their academic and behavioral success (Johnston & Chronis-Tuscano, 2015).

2. We buy into the stigmatized version of ADHD

When we take the deficit-based approach, believing our children aren't capable of certain things because they have ADHD, we buy into the stigmatized version of ADHD, not the real-life version.

This stigmatized version can bring about all sorts of negative feelings in our children, including shame, isolation, and embarrassment, and our children will start to have a lower outlook on their own lives and feel less capable (Johnston & Chronis-Tuscano, 2015).

3. **We don't advocate for our children as much**

When we believe that our children's ADHD can't be changed and adapted, and our children can't grow and learn, we are less likely to advocate for them. For example, we might not fight as hard to get them the support they need in school, as we assume that nothing will help. We might also continue to struggle with their behaviors at home, believing that whatever we do, it won't change how our children behave (Johnston & Chronis-Tuscano, 2015).

If you're reading this book, I can confidently say that you don't want these outcomes for your son. So, let's talk about the alternative: seeing ADHD as a neurodiversity and developing a growth mindset.

Growth mindset is a concept developed by American psychologist Carol Dweck. She believed that people can have one of two mindsets: a fixed mindset, or a growth mindset, and the mindset you have determines everything in life, from what you achieve to how you see yourself. The fixed mindset sits alongside the deficit-based model; it's the belief that the capabilities we are born with are fixed and can't be altered. So, for your son with ADHD, taking a fixed mindset would mean believing that he won't ever learn how to manage his ADHD symptoms. In contrast, a growth mindset is when you believe that everything is changeable and adaptable—that your son can learn new skills, grow, and adapt.

Let's look at some of the key differences between these two perspectives in the way people approach difficulties:

	Fixed Mindset	**Growth Mindset**
Facing Challenges	Shy away from & avoid challenges, automatically assuming that you will fail	Relish a challenge & embrace it
Overcoming Obstacles	Giving up quickly, often before you have given 100%	Persevering, even when faced with difficulties
Putting in Effort	Not recognizing the importance of effort, and quitting early	Seeing the power of effort & consistency to achieve your goals
Managing Criticism	Only hearing criticism as failure and not using the constructive feedback	Using the criticism to learn and grow
Responding to Others' Success	Feeling threatened by others' success	Feeling inspired by others' success and using it to help you grow

(Street, 2021).

Now, I want you to ask yourself—what mindset do you have? How might this be influencing your son? When I first started learning about mindsets, the idea of a growth vs. a fixed mindset hit me hard. I recognized that I was limiting my son, Max, so much, simply by believing that he couldn't learn and grow. When I started to develop a growth mindset, everything changed for my son, and it can for yours, too. So, let's explore how exactly you can foster a growth mindset. Then, in Chapter 5, I'll talk about how you can encourage a growth mindset in your son, too.

Step-by-Step Guide to Developing a Growth Mindset Towards ADHD

OK, let's get straight into it. To develop a growth mindset towards your son's ADHD, you need to do the following.

Step 1: Become an Expert in All Things ADHD

Take the time to truly get to know ADHD and understand how it influences your son. This involves understanding how he may differ from neurotypical children, and why this is (i.e., the differences in his brain), and start to understand neurodiversity from your son's experience.

Guess what? You're already doing step 1 just by reading this book! Seeing ADHD as a neurodiversity and not a disorder is what this book is all about, and as you work through it, I'll encourage you to explore your son's differences and how they impact him. So, you're already part of the way there!

Step 2: Find Your Son's Superpowers

Learn to look out for and recognize your son's strengths and the so-called "superpowers" that his ADHD gives him (because trust me, there are many!). Once you learn to look at the positive aspects of his ADHD diagnosis, the negative sides that may have consumed you in the past will start to fall away.

In Chapter 8, I'll focus on identifying your son's superpowers and showing him how his strengths can help him. So, stay tuned!

Step 3: Arm Yourself with Effective Parenting Strategies

When you arm yourself with effective parenting strategies, you'll begin to see how your son can adapt and change when given the right tools. The strategies that you'll need at your disposal are:

- Emotional regulation strategies
- Sensory overstimulation strategies
- Strategies for coping at school

- Strategies for developing practical skills like problem-solving and social skills

Again, as you work through the chapters of this book, I'll provide guidance on each of these sets of strategies and step-by-steps on how to implement them with your son, so sit back and keep reading!

Part of developing a growth mindset towards your son's ADHD is recognizing that there are many treatment options available to give him a helping hand and allow him to reach for everything he sets his sights on. However, you'll know as well as I do that it's not always easy understanding which treatment options will help, and which might hinder. Let's talk through some of the most effective options available, so you can find possibilities that work for your son.

Understanding Treatment Options

As a parent of a child with ADHD, treatment options can seem like a minefield. There are so many options, and options within those options, so it's tricky knowing which road to go down.

Before getting started on this section, it's important that you know one thing: this section is for informational purposes only. Each child with ADHD is different, and so the treatment options that work for one may not work for another. It would be unethical and wrong for me to recommend treatment options for your son based on what's worked for Max. So, you won't get any advice here. Instead, I'll tell you all of the options, some scary statistics, and the research on how effective each treatment option is, so you can make the judgment for yourself on which is most suitable for your son.

Now, let's get to the nitty gritty: what treatment options are out there? In truth, there are so many that I would have to write a separate book entirely to cover them all. Some are more common (and evidence-backed) than others. Here's a quick snapshot of treatment statistics in the US:

> **7/10 children receive at least two or three types of main treatments.**
>
> These main treatments include **medication, support at school, or psychosocial treatment**.
>
> - 9/10 children with ADHD receive ADHD medication in their lives.
> - 9/10 children with ADHD receive accommodations at school or other forms of school support.
> - 6/10 children with ADHD receive psychosocial treatment (3/10 parent-delivered behavior therapy, 4/10 social skills training, 3/10 peer interventions, and 2/10 CBT.)
> - 1/10 children with ADHD receive neurofeedback.
> - 2/10 children with ADHD take dietary supplements.
>
> Only 7% of children with ADHD have never received one of these main treatment options.

Centers for Disease Control and Prevention (2018)

Now, let's go over some of these main treatment options and other common alternative options. We'll cover:

- Stimulant medications
- Parental & child behavioral treatments
- Non-traditional strategies (like healthy eating, exercise, and outdoor activities)

STIMULANT MEDICATIONS

Stimulant medications are one of the most common treatment options for boys with ADHD, and they're often the first port of call when a child first receives an ADHD diagnosis. Research shows that 71% of children with an

ADHD diagnosis in one school were receiving stimulant medication treatment—71%!

So, medication is a very common form of treatment, and this is likely due to its reported effectiveness in kids with ADHD. Past research has found that stimulant drugs are highly effective at reducing ADHD symptoms; much more so than behavioral treatments (Jensen, 1999).

Yet despite the reported benefits of stimulant medications, there are some drawbacks, too. For starters, like with any medication, stimulants have side effects. Some of the most common are:

- Appetite changes (often reduced appetite)
- Increased aggression
- Headaches, gastrointestinal issues, and other physical symptoms (Kamal et al., 2018).

There is also limited evidence on the long-term benefits of meds for children with ADHD, and there is the potential for misuse. What's more, the weight increase often seen in kids taking stimulants can have big detrimental effects on their BMI and overall health (Vitulano et al., 2022).

BEHAVIOR MANAGEMENT PARENT TRAINING

Behavior management parent training is a form of therapy or training that we parents can take with or without our sons. It is often offered to parents of children who are showing "behavior problems" such as disruption, impulsivity, and hyperactivity in the classroom.

The aim of behavior management parent training is to equip parents with strategies so that they know how to manage their children's behaviors effectively and respond in ways that naturally bring about what are deemed more "acceptable" behaviors.

Some of the most common options are:
- Parent management therapy
- Behavioral parent training
- Parent-child interaction therapy (PCIT)

Research shows that behavior management parent trainings like those listed above can improve children's behavior, aid their positive social development so they can behave more similarly to their peers, and also reduce parental stress. Perhaps the most key change of all—this form of treatment has shown to strengthen parents' bond with their children (Vitulano et al., 2022).

However, there are also problems with this approach. Firstly, the research into these training programs isn't particularly strong—most often, studies only assess a handful of children, so this raises a question of whether the training is beneficial for the wider population, or just the select few. What's more, the positive changes don't appear to stick around for long, so you may need to keep hunting for alternative treatment options as your child develops. And finally, one study found that behavior management parent training didn't do much to manage children's core ADHD symptoms, such as externalizing behaviors (Zwi et al., 2011).

Non-Traditional Strategies

Doctors and other health professionals also often recommended trying a range of non-traditional strategies to support children with ADHD. These generally involve lifestyle changes that are supposed to reduce children's stress and support their development. The most common ones that are recommended are:

- **A healthy, balanced diet**

Diet and ADHD is a much-debated topic, particularly when it comes to how much sugar children are eating. While many parents are led to believe that sugar can cause ADHD, it's important to be clear that there is no evidence for this. Likewise, changing your son's diet won't stop his ADHD symptoms altogether, but it may make them more manageable.

So, what should we be trying to give our children less of? Research from back in 2010 found a link between ADHD symptoms and the Western diet; namely, calorific diets with high levels of fat and sugar. But the evidence is mixed on the precise foods that may heighten ADHD symptoms, so the jury is still out on this one.

- **Regular exercise**

Regular exercise can help children with ADHD burn off steam, which can be particularly beneficial if your son struggles with social skills, impulsivity, and focusing for prolonged periods due to ADHD. Some research suggests that spending as little as twenty minutes outside in nature can boost an ADHD child's concentration.

Experts generally recommend that children spend at least sixty minutes engaging in forms of moderate or intense exercise daily, such as riding their bike, gymnastics, soccer, and so on.

- **A set sleep schedule**

The research on getting a good night's sleep for a child with ADHD is extremely promising. For example, it shows that getting even as little as thirty minutes more sleep a night could be enough to reduce children's impulsivity and restlessness.

Unfortunately though, while this strategy is good in theory, in reality, many children with ADHD find it difficult to settle and fall asleep. In fact, around 50 - 95% of children with neurodevelopmental disorders (including ADHD) have difficulties with sleeping (Villines, 2021).

However, the best way to start is to help your son develop good sleep habits, including ensuring he goes to bed at the same time every night, that his bedroom stays cool and as dark as possible, and that he stays away from screens and stimulating things, such as games, in the last few hours before bed (WebMD Editorial Contributors, 2023). I'll talk more about this in Chapter 6, where you'll get all the tips and tools you'll need to help your son form healthy habits, including a consistent bedtime schedule.

Chapter Takeaways

- **ADHD isn't straightforward.** The history behind ADHD is complex, and the information on ADHD remains confusing, even now. So, if you find yourself getting muddled and confused, you're not alone!
- **More boys show ADHD symptoms than girls.** ADHD is diagnosed in boys more often than in girls, but this tends to level out in adulthood. One reason for this may be due to the disparities in the symptoms that boys and girls with ADHD present with.
- **ADHD varies from child to child.** Your son may have a completely different presentation to Max, or another child in their class. Get to know your son's individual presentation so you can understand what he struggles most with.
- **ADHD is a neurodiversity, NOT a disorder.** Seeing our sons as different rather than deficient, and ensuring we practice a growth mindset rather than a fixed one, can help our sons reach their full potential and recognize their strengths.
- **There are many treatment options to choose from.** Each treatment option comes with pros and cons. It's important to know the options available and to make the choice that you feel is best for your son.

Chapter 2: Building a Supportive Home for Your Son

"Every child has a different learning style and pace. Each child is unique, not only capable of learning but also capable of succeeding."
– Robert John Meehan

I've talked a lot about children with ADHD showing difficult behaviors in school, but it's important to give a shout-out to all of you parents who don't experience this. It's common for children with ADHD to get on well in one setting and not in another (Lopes, 2023). So, your son may struggle predominantly at school, *or* he may face most of his troubles at home.

One thing that I often tell parents of children with ADHD is this: your son WILL show difficult behaviors at home. Why? Because it's where he feels safest in the world. It may be infuriating for you that you seem to get the brunt of all his behavior. And it may be hurtful. Often, when our sons act aggressively or are dysregulated at home, we're quick to ask ourselves, "What did I do wrong?" But the answer is likely nothing. You didn't do anything wrong. Instead, your son reacted in this way because he feels safe to do so.

Of course, behaviors like hitting out, insulting us and their siblings, and screaming at us aren't the best way to handle the situation, but it's good that ADHD boys feel able to show their emotions at home. Once you begin to see your child's emotional expressions as a good thing—as a sign of trust and a feeling of safety—you can begin to work with your son's behaviors and build a supportive home environment that helps him develop strategies to cope with these.

Now, let's start really laying out how you can create a supportive space at home so your son feels accepted and understood.

Creating a Supportive Home Environment

The home environment can be the third parent we didn't know existed. According to the Reggio Emilia Approach, an educational philosophy, the home environment can act as a child's "third teacher", helping them learn about themselves and others.

The Reggio Emilia philosophy sees children as competent and capable and suggests that children have an inner drive to explore their environment. You and I both know this is the case with kids with ADHD—their desire to explore never stops!

The Reggio Emilia Approach is child-centered, meaning it holds children at the heart. When we follow this philosophy, we help our children independently find their interests and gain autonomy through self-directed learning. It involves setting up their environment in a way that allows them to make their own choices. While we will redirect them, this will be done using empathy and understanding, not punishment and yelling.

The Reggio Emilia Approach may be particularly beneficial for children with ADHD as it helps to satisfy their hyperactivity and impulsivity in a way that also respects others, allowing them to learn how to get it right when they may often feel as though they're getting it wrong.

What does this approach mean for your home environment?

Well, when we say the home environment is the "third teacher" or an additional parent, we're acknowledging the part our environment plays in our children's mood, behavior, and relationships. We absorb everything in our environment and reflect it back as a behavior, and so do our children.

So, ask yourself:

- What message does my home environment send my son? Is it a place where he can be calm, playful, or independent? Or is it a chaotic, stressful space that reflects in his behavior?
- Is my home environment setting my son up for success, regulation, and connection? Or is it likely to be sending him into a dysregulated, disconnected mood?

Once you've got your answers, let's move onto two simple tips to make your home feel calm and supportive for your son.

TIP #1: DECLUTTER YOUR HOME

Decluttering your home is a great way to help calm not just your son with ADHD but also yourself. Despite the research suggesting this very effect, some people are still skeptical. So, let's consider it this way: you walk into your workplace, and there are items everywhere; you've got two desktops, five notepads, two staplers, Post-it notes everywhere, and to top it all off, seven keyboards. How do you think you'd feel walking into a space like that? Would you be able to concentrate? Would you be feeling cool as a cucumber? Tell me that wouldn't be stressful.

While our homes may not be cluttered to that degree, even small, cluttered spaces can be overwhelming for our sons with ADHD. Clutter is visually stressful because the boys have to process excess stimuli, which can overload their brains pretty quickly. It also distracts them by pulling their attention away from where it's *supposed* to be, which makes each task harder to complete. Then there's the fact that clutter makes everything more difficult to find, which becomes stressful and overwhelming, particularly in situations like the morning school rush.

Research shows that clutter can have a big impact on all of our brains, not only our sons with ADHD. Excess items in our surroundings can lead to:

- Difficulties focusing
- Trouble processing information
- Lower general performance
- More stress

(ADD Crusher, 2017)

So, decluttering our homes is a must to try to ensure our sons with ADHD are as comfortable and relaxed as possible when they're at home. But there's a slight caveat to this, and you may have already been asking this very question: Where am I going to find the time to declutter? I hear you. Gone are the days before you were a parent when you could declutter your whole home in one weekend. Now, we have to work smarter, not harder, and make the most of the time we've got. So, try to set aside 30 - 60 minutes a day and work room-by-room. Make a list of each space you have to declutter, then get to work on them one by one, ensuring you finish one first before moving on to the next.

Trust me, as soon as you're done, you'll begin to notice the changes in your son (and yourself!).

TIP #2: CREATE "GO" SPACES

I used to say "no" to Max more times than I cared to count every single day, especially when we were out of the house. I desperately wanted to create spaces where he could be himself, do his own thing independently, and not have me constantly setting boundaries and telling him "no". That's when I heard of this thing called "go" spaces.

"Go" spaces are spaces where you don't have to say "no"—where nothing is off limits for your son, and he can do as he pleases. Yes, that means goodbye to the "don't touch"s and the "get down"s, and even the "stop that"s. Creating a "go" space in your home allows you, your son, and the whole family to relax, as your son has the space to move around, explore, and meet his own needs. Plus, you'll feel at peace knowing he won't injure himself, and you don't have to worry about him.

While a "go" space will look different in every home, there are three key things to keep in mind when creating a "go" space in your home:

1. **Focus on Safety**: If you know he's safe, you don't have to worry about him. So, check the space you've chosen as the "go" space for anything that would be unsafe. Getting down to your son's eye level can really help during this stage!
2. **Encourage Independence:** All "go" spaces should encourage independence as it enables your son to help himself without needing your assistance or "okay." For example, put materials like coloring pencils out so they're easily accessible; put other materials away and out of sight.
3. **Prioritize Play:** Creating playful spaces for your son can really help him feel comfortable at home and can help him blow off the steam that he likely stores up at school. This could be a climbing wall, a foam pit, a bouncer, or even building blocks.

Not only does creating a "go" space help your son feel more independent, but it'll also make him feel more encouraged and capable, and give him better self-esteem and a sense of agency. Plus, you'll feel like you're on the same team, which can make a nice change from all of the times when you have to say "no!"

But here's the thing: no matter how many "go" spaces you create at home, your son spends 32.5 hours a week at school—around 9% of his life up until the age of eighteen. So, it's important for him to feel supported at school, too. To do this, you need to master the foolproof way of collaborating with schools. More on this next.

Foolproof Way of Collaborating with Schools

Collaborating with your son's school is no mean feat, and that's not by any means blaming his teacher. Schools are hectic, busy environments, and with the way they are currently run, the teacher-to-children ratio is shockingly inadequate. Yet, this doesn't take away from the importance of collaborating with schools to support your son with ADHD.

In fact, research looking into this very thing stresses the importance of teachers and parents dedicating their energy and time to supporting a child with ADHD. By collaborating, you can share important information and experiences, help educate teachers on how to support your son in the best way, and brainstorm new strategies together (Christenson & Sheridan, 2001; Henderson & Mapp, 2022). Remember, you know your son best, so if you can find a way to communicate your knowledge to your son's teacher, you're onto a winner. Here's how to do it:

- **Take the Lead:** Teachers are extremely busy, so you can't assume that they will be focusing on supporting your son 100% of the time. If you want to communicate, take the lead. Initiate and maintain active communication with your child's teacher so you can make decisions together and exchange ideas (Braley, 2012).
- **Try Different Forms of Communication:** If you can't get through to your son's teacher via email, ask them whether there is another form of communication they prefer. Give them a call, book an in-person meeting, and if they're really unresponsive, go above their head and speak to the principal. Your son has a right to access support, so ensure you're being heard (Taylor, Smiley & Richards, 2009).

- **Be Honest and Offer Support:** Ensure you keep an honest, open, and respectful relationship, and offer your son's teacher your support whenever you can. For example, provide additional resources if your son needs them or share any guidance that you have received with his teacher. Approaching collaboration in this way helps to build trust, which can be invaluable when it comes to supporting your son.
- **Remember, You're a Team:** It's not you vs. your son's teacher, even though it can feel like it sometimes. Remember that you have a shared interest—to ensure your son learns effectively and thrives in school. Use this to create a team around your son (Welch & Sheridan, 1995).

If you've been trying and trying to get the support your son needs but to no avail, you're not alone. Many, many parents of children with ADHD experience the same problems. The school system is nowhere near perfect, especially for kids with additional needs. In moments where you're fighting and struggling, it's easy to feel alone. That's where the help of like-minded parents can come in *reaaaal* handy.

Filling Your Social Calendar with Like-Minded Parents

I've said this already, and I'll say it again because I want you to really, truly take it in: parenting a child with ADHD is HARD. There are many times when it can feel lonely (speaking from experience here!). When you hit one of those times, you know what really helps? Having someone in your corner who understands, such as another parent whose child has ADHD.

Research shows that we all benefit from social support, every single one of us. But the benefits are especially evident for those of us who have a child with ADHD. In fact, recent research shows that when we have a supportive social network, not only do our stress levels go down, but we also feel happier (Johnston et al., 2012. Why? When we don't feel like we're all on our own, it stops us from feeling like we're going crazy.

So, as you go through the ups and downs of an ADHD diagnosis for your son and the journey to supporting him in the best way possible, prioritize filling your calendar with exciting social occasions with other parents who "get it". Here are some places you can find great parents like this:

- **Online forums like Reddit.** Seriously, check these out. They're brimming with parents' experiences of having a child with ADHD; the good, the bad, and the downright hilarious.
- **Support groups.** There are support groups for pretty much anything nowadays, and that's because they are a great way to meet like-minded people. Try researching your local mental health clinics, community centers, and also online directories, like Children and Adults with Attention Deficit Hyperactivity Disorder, for guidance.
- **School support groups.** Sometimes, schools where there are high levels of need will host support groups. Keep on top of the school's calendar and ensure you're aware if any of these are going on.
- **Online webinars.** If you find it too difficult to get out and meet parents, why not try online? There are so many webinars, many of them free, to support parents of children with additional needs.
- **Referrals from mental health professionals.** If your son is seeing a therapist or other mental health professional, ask them if they know of any organizations or groups where you can meet like-minded parents. They will often have all the information on the local resources you need!
- **Mental health organizations.** Check out the big mental health organizations like NAMI and Parent to Parent USA to find helpful resources and numbers to call to start chatting with other parents.

My wife and I were feeling really bogged down by Max's ADHD diagnosis around a year in. We spoke to the special education director at Max's school, and she gave us a couple of websites to check out to look at parent meetups. We went to a few and found it such a relief to know that it wasn't just us. Plus, we found some parents who were further down the ADHD journey than us, and they gave us tons of great tips, many of which I'm passing on to you in this book!

There was one parent in particular, Ellie, whose son had severe sensory difficulties that made it incredibly hard for him to engage in school or anything outside of the home environment. She helped us to understand Max's sensory needs and ways we could help him cope. So, thanks to Ellie, that's what I'm discussing next—uncovering and addressing your son's sensory triggers.

Chapter Takeaways

- **Your son WILL act differently at home.** Your son's behavior may be very different at home than in school, and that's okay. Your son acting up at home could be a sign that he feels safe enough to let go of his pent-up frustration.
- **Creating supportive spaces for your son is VITAL.** Your son may feel unsupported most of the time, especially at school where it's hard for him to receive the attention he may need. Use the Reggio Emilia Approach to create a home space that encourages learning, autonomy, and exploration.
- **Decluttering your home makes a BIG difference to your son.** Reducing the number of visual distractors and items your son will have to process can go a long way in making him feel relaxed in his surroundings. Plus, a clutter-free space will likely help him focus.
- **You can't beat school collaboration.** Collaborating with your son's school can help him get the support he needs, which will allow him to learn as much as possible. Ensure you build a

relationship with the school based on honesty, open communication, and resource sharing.

- **Get dates with like-minded parents in your diary.** You need to fill your world with parents who understand what you're going through. Seek support from the resources around you and share experiences with parents who know the score.

* * *

To help implement the strategies in this chapter, please scan the QR code below to access your first free bonus toolkit: **The ADHD School Planner.**

This is an all-inclusive school planner for boys with ADHD, including editable files, activity logs, schedules, planners, trackers for assignments and grades, and checklists to help them stay organized and on top of their schoolwork.

Chapter 3: Uncovering and Addressing Sensory Triggers

"Behind every young child who believes in himself is a parent who believed first."
– Matthew L. Jacobson

Your childhood memories of the beach may be filled with fun and excitement, but for a second, try to imagine something different.

You've gone into the sea to explore on your own, but you've gone slightly too far. Before you know it, a wave hits you, and the weight pushes you over. Just as you're recovering from the wave, another one hits. And again. And again.

It's an unpleasant thought, right? Well, this type of sensation isn't unfamiliar to many children with ADHD (Bijlenga et al., 2017). In fact, some ADHD kids may experience this almost daily in the form of overstimulation.

If you've been around the ADHD block for a while, you've likely heard of the term "sensory overload" or "overstimulation". If you're unsure exactly what sensory overload is, the exact definition of each is:

- **Sensory overload:** "when your sense of sound, touch, taste, smell, and sight take in more information than your brain is able to process" (Queensland Health, 2022).

- **Overstimulation:** "a state of feeling overwhelmed by your surrounding environment or situation" (Green, 2022).

Sensory overload and overstimulation are similar, but not the same thing. Overstimulation occurs as a result of sensory overload. So, sensory overload is the trigger, overstimulation is the reaction.

Sensory overload is particularly common in children, as their brains are still developing, which means they haven't developed the ability to manage incoming sensory stimuli. However, kids with ADHD are even more prone to sensory overload because they:

- Struggle to regulate their emotions
- Hyperfocus on their environment
- Are impulsive
- Are often sensitive to light, sound, touch, smells, and tastes.

As sensory overload happens when their brains become overwhelmed by receiving so many inputs from the environment, these factors all increase a child's risk of experiencing sensory overload. Children who struggle with anxiety, post-traumatic stress disorder, autism, or other sensory processing disorders may experience sensory overload for similar reasons.

Let's get one thing clear—just as ADHD is different in each child, so do the causes of sensory overload and a child's reaction to overstimulation. For example, some children may be particularly sensitive to light, which makes going into a mall or superstore where they have bright, white lights overstimulating. For another child, clothing that feels scratchy or labels that irritate the skin may be particularly overwhelming. However, while the experiences do differ, there are some common sensory triggers that cause sensory overload, as well as common patterns of behavior when a child is overstimulated. More on this next.

Sensory Overload: The Common Sensory Triggers

While the triggers vary from child to child, research has found similar patterns in children with ADHD. The most common triggers are:

1. **Touch:** Sudden touch, or touch that is too light or firm, can cause sensory overload. For example, people with ADHD may describe light touch as being "itchy" or like their skin is crawling.
2. **Smell:** Strong scents, such as from perfumes, fragrances, or food, may feel physically uncomfortable if your child has a heightened sense of smell.
3. **Sound:** Sudden, loud, or many sounds at once may cause someone with ADHD to become overwhelmed. Sounds, particularly if a child is hypersensitive to sounds, may cause them stress. Social situations where multiple conversations are going on at once can also feel stressful for those with ADHD if they're sensitive to sounds.
4. **Sight:** Flashing lights or harsh, luminescent lights may cause some children with ADHD to become overwhelmed. This is common in places like superstores or malls.
5. **Taste:** Strong flavors or spiciness can lead to sensory overload, as well as certain food temperatures.
6. **Texture:** Certain food textures can bring about overstimulation in some ADHDers. For example, some people struggle with crunchy candies or raw vegetables, typically preferring soft foods. Scratchy or restrictive clothing also falls into this category, and this, too, can cause overstimulation.

(Mae, 2023)

When a child with ADHD feels overstimulated, they may become emotionally dysregulated, causing them to shut down, lash out, or become irritable. For neurotypical people, overstimulation can look like an overreaction. For our ADHD kids, overstimulation can feel like an utter state of overwhelm—like every piece of information they're processing is too much, and they have no control of their surroundings.

They can feel sudden tension or irritability, or it can feel like the world is moving too fast for them. Some children experiencing overstimulation may get up and leave the room without warning, or put their hands over their ears or eyes to make the onslaught of information stop. For others, overstimulation may mean they zone out from their environment, making them feel far away and distant from their current situation.

Overstimulation can and often does feel entirely different for every child. While it may not feel painful for some, it feels incredibly physically uncomfortable for most.

How Does Overstimulation Affect Children with ADHD?

Overstimulation typically poses various difficulties for children with ADHD. It's physically, psychologically, and emotionally uncomfortable, which isn't pleasant. But there are bigger implications than this. Children who often experience overstimulation may struggle to concentrate or become overwhelmed in lots of situations, such as in a classroom or public setting. If they're unable to concentrate or they feel stressed, they're less likely to socialize or be aware of their surroundings. For example, if a child with hypersensitivity to sound is in a classroom, and the teacher instructs the students to work in groups, this child may become overwhelmed by lots of people talking at once, causing them to have to sit out of the group work. This can have a negative impact on their social relationships.

What's more, we've already talked about how emotional reactivity can be a problem for children with ADHD. If they're constantly becoming overwhelmed and stressed by their surroundings, they're far more likely to act on impulse, either by lashing out or trying to leave the environment.

As such, overstimulation can affect children's school lives, relationships, stress levels, and behaviors. It may also make them highly avoidant of certain environments, which can cause loneliness and isolation.

So, as parents, we need to learn how to weather the storm of overstimulation and help our sons identify their sensory triggers.

Teaching Your Son to Recognize His Sensory Triggers

As I've already established, sensory overload and overstimulation can have a huge impact on a child's life. So, in order to support your son with overstimulation, it's important to teach him to recognize his own sensory triggers. First, you need to get a good idea of what those may be.

Let's work through each sensory trigger in turn—if you're not sure what sensory triggers your son has, look out for the boxes at the top of each section. These include questions to ask yourself to help you identify whether the sensory trigger affects your son.

VISUAL HYPERSENSITIVITY

- Does your son become overwhelmed in brightly-lit environments like superstores?
- Does your son cover his eyes in places with lights or sunlight?
- Does he seem overwhelmed or agitated in visually busy spaces?
- Does your son become irritated or overwhelmed in cluttered spaces?
- Does he avoid places that are visually stimulating, like amusement parks or crowded malls?
- Does your son squint, rub his eyes, or blink excessively in response to visual stimuli like lights?
- Does your son struggle when phones, TVs, or computers are too bright?
- Does your son's mood change in relation to the brightness of the environment?

Just as a quick recap, visual hypersensitivity involves being overly sensitive to things we see, such as lights, sunlight, or crowded spaces where there is a lot going on in our vision. Here are some quick ways you can help your son if he struggles with visual hypersensitivity:

1. **Dim the lighting at home**

Your son may find bright lights overwhelming. So, if he does, a quick and easy way to reduce the likelihood of him becoming overstimulated at home is to dim the lights or switch to lamp lighting instead of overhead lights. Also, consider swapping fluorescent bulbs with dimmer, colored ones—these are often less intense, and so have a less harsh effect on the eyes.

2. **Buy him glasses**

If your son wears glasses, ensure his prescription is up to date and his glasses have anti-glare lenses—these will help protect his eyes from unnecessary glare. Keeping a pair of sunglasses in the car or in your bag can also help on sunny days.

Alternatively, kit your son out with transition glasses—these act as both prescription glasses and sunglasses, automatically changing based on the brightness of his environment.

3. **Rethink your home decor**

If you love maximalist interior design, I'm sorry to say that mishmashes of colors, patterns, and shapes may overstimulate a child with visual hypersensitivity.

Even if maximalism isn't your style, go around your home and check your decor. Are there lots of bright colors? Are there lots of items cluttering up the spaces? Ensure your home is as clutter free as possible, particularly your son's room. This will help him to feel calm and regulated at home.

Auditory Hypersensitivity

- Does your son put his hands over his ears when there is a loud or sudden noise?
- Does he complain about loud noises?
- Does he become overwhelmed in crowded, noisy environments?
- Does he attempt to avoid loud environments, such as cinemas, concerts, or fireworks displays?
- Does your son struggle to concentrate in environments with multiple sounds or conversations?
- Is your son sensitive to particular pitches or frequencies of music?
- Does your son struggle to sleep when there are noises?
- Does your son have headaches or ear pain after being in noisy environments?

We often can't control the sounds around us, so a sensitivity to sounds can be particularly tricky for kids with ADHD. However, there are certain steps we can take as parents to support our kids if they're hypersensitive to sounds; these include the items below.

1. Designate Time for Quiet Activities

Carving out some time within your son's schedule for quiet activities can make more of a difference than you might initially think. As school can be so loud and busy, it's vital that our sons have a safe, calming space to come back to when they're at home, and for boys who struggle with auditory sensitivity, ensuring it's filled with quiet activities is a must. Here are some examples of great quiet activities for auditory sensitive kids:

- Reading
- Drawing
- Journaling
- DIY crafts
- Sticker books
- Bird watching
- Cooking/baking

- Storytelling
- Gardening
- Yoga or stretching
- Painting
- Sensory bins (bins filled with sensory materials like sand, rice, beans, and so on).
- Playdough or clay

Base your choices on your son's preferences, and see how you get on! Part of this will be trial and error—some will work to keep him entertained, and others may go wrong. But that's part of the fun, right?

2. Use White Noise Machines, Low-Gain Hearing Aids, or Noise-Canceling Headphones

For a child with noise sensitivity, practical solutions are a must. Luckily, there are quite a few options to help children manage their noise sensitivity (far more than back in my day!). The first option is a white noise machine. According to research, steady background noises can improve a person with ADHD's focus and concentration as they can block out other distracting noises (Angwin et al., 2017). White noise also supposedly stimulates the production of dopamine, a so-called "happy" hormone, which makes it a great addition to a study space or cool-down zone (Rausch, Bauch & Bunzeck, 2014)!

Then there are low-gain hearing aids—these are typically used for people who find processing conversations difficult when there is background noise as they enhance speech while suppressing background noise (HearSay, n.d.). Low-gain hearing aids were originally developed for people with auditory processing disorder, but can also be helpful for sensory processing disorders, ADHD, and autism. Really, they're recommended for any child who struggles to process sounds or has problems with inattentiveness and lack of focus.

And finally, one of Max's personal favorites, noise-canceling headphones. These are so handy because you can take them with you wherever you go. They can be used as a precautionary measure if your son's hearing is particularly sensitive or in situations where you know there are going to be loud sounds, like fireworks displays, concerts, etc. Max couldn't manage without them nowadays!

3. Consider Noisiness During Outings

It's not always possible to predict loud sounds, and that's OK. It's important that our children know that this is a natural part of the world around them. However, as part of supporting them as best as we can, it's our job to make sure that they are equipped to deal with difficult, noisy situations when they arise. Rather than approaching the situation with anxiety, ensure you pack your son's headphones, hearing aids, or other supportive object to make the noise more bearable.

TOUCH HYPERSENSITIVITY

- Does your son experience discomfort or become overwhelmed by light physical contact?
- Do certain fabrics or textures of clothes irritate or dysregulate your son?
- Does your son express discomfort when there are tags, labels, or uncomfortable seams in his clothes?
- Does your son avoid activities that involve touch, like sand, paint, or other forms of messy play?
- Does your son dislike or seek out hugs, cuddles, and squeezes?
- Does your son dislike any form of physical affection or touch?
- Have you noticed your son reacts in extreme ways to minor cuts, scrapes, and injuries?
- Does your son become overwhelmed or dysregulated in crowded spaces?
- Does your son struggle when he feels too hot or too cold?

Touch hypersensitivity is a tricky one because it's not always obvious when your child is sensitive to tactile things like their clothes, crowds, or physical touch. Some children may become extremely dysregulated when you try to hug them, while others may struggle in silence, becoming more and more overwhelmed until they lose their temper at something completely unrelated.

If you're worried that your son may struggle with touch hypersensitivity, here are a couple of things you can do:

1. **Try deep pressure like a firm massage or a big "bear hug" & weighted items**

It's often light, scratchy touches that children with ADHD can't stand. If this is the case for your son, try offering deep-pressure touches instead. This could be in the form of a firm massage or swapping a normal hug for a big bear hug where you squeeze each other really tightly.

A real lifesaver for many parents I've spoken to with a son with ADHD is a weighted blanket. These are like regular blankets but they've got weights inside, making them really heavy. When a child is feeling dysregulated, the weighted blanket can help calm them down, as the deep pressure actually triggers the release of the "happy" hormone dopamine.

One other technique that has worked wonders on Max is the Wilbarger brushing protocol (Beck, 2023). This is a form of deep pressure brushing therapy that involves applying firm pressure from a soft-bristled brush to your son's skin. This sounds a little strange and wacky, but bear with me here—it's a tool that many occupational therapists use. Here's how it goes:

1. Make sure your son is in a completely calm, comfortable state, and invite him to lie down on a hard surface, such as a wooden or carpeted floor.
2. Get your soft-bristled brush, like a hairbrush, and apply firm but gentle pressure onto your son's skin using the brush. Start with his arms, then brush downwards toward his hands, and then move onto his legs, brushing down towards his feet.
3. Make sure you use long, even strokes, and check in with your son to make sure the pressure is okay. Stay away from spots where the skin is sensitive, like his face or stomach.
4. Once you've done over your son's arms and legs once, do it again, keeping a consistent pressure and rhythm as you go.
5. Keep an eye on how your son responds to this and ask him whether it feels comfortable. If your son struggles to articulate his bodily feelings, keep an eye on his behavior and regulation after this activity. Then you can identify whether it's calming or dysregulating.

TASTE HYPERSENSITIVITY

- Is your son what most people call a "picky" or "fussy" eater?
- Does your son seem dysregulated after meals?
- Is your son reluctant to try new foods?
- Does your son show a preference for bland foods?
- Does your son become overwhelmed or dysregulated when food is too hot or too cold?
- Does his mood change before or after mealtimes?
- Does your son tend to gag, spit out, or retch when trying new or strongly flavored foods?
- Does he seem particularly sensitive to particular tastes, like spiciness, bitterness, or sourness?

Is your son what most people would call a "picky eater"? There may be several reasons for this. He may be hypersensitive to taste, meaning he struggles with certain tastes. Sometimes, when kids are highly sensitive to tastes, they may say that a food is "hurting" them or feels really uncomfortable—this could be due to hypersensitivity.

Another reason why your son may be a picky eater is because children with ADHD supposedly naturally crave sugary foods to increase their levels of dopamine (Olivardio, 2024). This makes sense, as research shows that children with ADHD typically have lower levels of dopamine. This may mean they turn their nose up at non-sugary foods like, say, vegetables, always requesting sugary and processed foods.

So, what can you do if your child struggles with taste hypersensitivity?

1. Make it fun with "snake tests"

Snake tests are a great, fun way to get your son excited about trying new foods. This is particularly helpful for younger kids aged six and below, but it can work for older children if they are playful. A snake test starts with your son simply being near a new food. So, have it around the house, on the dinner table, on your plate, and so on. Get him familiar with the sight of it before you ever encourage him to taste it.

Then, get him comfortable with the food by getting him to handle it. What does it feel like? Is it squishy or hard? What happens when you press it in between your fingers? Allowing your son to explore new foods like this can help him feel more comfortable and familiar with it.

Then for the all-important "snake test". This involves giving the food a super-fast lick while, of course, pretending to be a snake! This will help give your son a taste of the food without fully committing to having it in his mouth. As he becomes more familiar with the food's taste, encourage him to place the food on his tongue for ten seconds, then eventually swallow a small bite.

The key to the "snake test" is to be patient. Let your son take as long as he needs to get comfortable with each stage before moving onto the next. It could take a few days or even weeks or months. However, it's worth it if he ends up liking a new, healthy food!

2. If at first, you don't succeed, try ten more times (or even eleven!)

Did you know that it takes us roughly twelve tries to identify if we like a particular food? As parents, we often offer up a food to our children once, twice, or perhaps three times. Once they've spat it up or thrown it on the floor three times, we assume that they don't like it.

However, research shows that we need repeated exposure to some foods, particularly those with a bitter taste, to acquire a taste for them. Of course, some foods, like sugary ones, are immediately pleasing to our taste buds. According to experts, this all goes back to our evolution— when food resources were scarce, we would eat any sugary foods we could find, as they were likely to provide the boost of energy we needed. At the same time, more bitter foods were more likely to be poisonous when we were scavenging, so we're generally more wary of foods like these.

This is where exposure comes in. Part of the reason why your son may not like a certain food or the flavor of that food is because it's unfamiliar. So, don't be disheartened if he continues to turn it down time after time. Keep going, and perhaps one day, if you combine it with the "snake test" technique, he'll become familiar with it.

SMELL HYPERSENSITIVITY

- Does your son show physical discomfort or overwhelm in environments with strong smells, such as perfume or incense stores, or restaurants?
- Does your son show an extreme dislike for certain smells?
- Can your son notice subtle smells in the environment that you can barely detect?
- Does your son struggle to concentrate when he's exposed to a strong smell?
- Does your son have a seemingly intense or extreme reaction to what you deem normal smells, such as food, deodorants, etc?
- Does your son wrinkle up his nose, sneeze, cough, or cover his nose when exposed to smelly environments?
- Does your son feel nauseous or dizzy or suffer from headaches when he's in environments with strong smells?

1. Organize "no scent" zones

When you have a child with smell hypersensitivity, your first decision may be to remove anything that overwhelms them from your home. So, you say goodbye to perfumes, air fresheners, certain strong-smelling foods, scented cleaning products, vinegar, flowering plants … the list could go on.

Completely removing these scented items from your home may not be necessary. Instead, you can organize "no scent" zones—places in the house where your son *knows* he's not going to feel overwhelmed by overpowering smells. For example, these places could be his bedroom and the bathroom. It can also be helpful to keep any chill-out zones free from uncomfortable smells so he can relax freely.

Then, in the other areas of the home, prepare him with strategies just like you would for the outside world. Not only does this give him a chance to experience what exposure might be like in small doses, but he can also practice using his coping strategies so he feels better equipped when he's outside of home.

2. Keep a pleasant smell close at hand

There's nothing worse than the anxiety of going to a new place, knowing that your son could begin to feel overwhelmed by the smells at any given time. So, as parents, we have to take action. We can't completely isolate our sons from unpleasant smells, but we can help them build strategies to manage these situations.

One of the best methods for this is carrying around a pleasant smell. So, say you're walking through a farmer's market, and they're cooking fish. Uh oh, you think. Your son hates the smell of fish. What are you going to do? Instead of panicking and pulling him away from there as quickly as possible for fear of him becoming overwhelmed, reach into your bag and grab the Tupperware container of his favorite smellies for him to sniff to block out the smell.

Here is a list of smellies that might work wonders for your son:

- Freshly sliced citrus fruit like lemon, orange, or lime.
- Your son's favorite essential oil. Lavender or peppermint are great as they are proven to have a relaxing effect, but you could also try vanilla and eucalyptus.
- Wax melts. These fit easily in Tupperware containers, and your son can pick his favorites to take with him for that day.
- Fresh herbs like basil or mint can also be really helpful, and you can get them straight out of your garden!
- Fresh ginger. This is another 100% natural item that has a very powerful smell.
- Cinnamon sticks. If your son loves cinnamon, cinnamon sticks can be a great smelly to carry around with you, and they're so small, you could fit them in your pocket!
- A lavender bag, like those that you can put in your sock drawer. Again, this can be slipped into a pocket and is perfect if your son prefers to be discreet.

TEXTURE HYPERSENSITIVITY

- Does your son show extreme discomfort or disgust with foods of certain textures, such as crunchy foods or raw vegetables?
- Does your son prefer to have foods of similar textures or have foods of different textures separate on his plate?
- Does your son seem dysregulated after meals?
- Does your son like objects that have a particular texture, such as smooth, symmetrical, or soft?
- Does your son report feeling itchy or uncomfortable when in contact with some textures?
- Does your son show extreme dislike of slimy or gritty textures?
- Does your son fear or avoid certain objects or items based on the way they feel?

Texture hypersensitivity is when, you guessed it, the feel of certain textures causes dysregulation. Certain food textures and scratchy or restrictive clothing causing overwhelm can fall into the category of texture hypersensitivity. To support your son with texture hypersensitivity, try the following.

1. Buying specialized clothing

Trust me, this is a no-brainer for kids with texture hypersensitivity. While back in your or my day there might not have been specialized clothing for kids with hypersensitivities like this, I'm pleased to say that our modern age has brought many such invaluable additions!

One of these is seamless socks. Seamless socks are exactly what they say on the tin— socks without seams. Gone are the days when your son had to turn his socks inside out to avoid the seams or forego socks altogether. With seamless socks, you won't have any of these issues. My favorite online store for seamless socks is Smart Knit Kids (www.smartknitkids.com). Check them out!

You can also now buy clothes that have sewn down seams, no labels at all, and even tops that provide compression or give a hug sensation for kids that love deep pressure.

The only downfall with these specialized clothes is that they can be expensive. If you're strapped for cash and can't afford these alternatives, you can simply get around things like labels by removing them. Also, giving your son Lycra or spandex clothes to wear under his school uniform can be a lifesaver, as this clothing provides deep pressure, which could help him feel calm throughout the day.

2. Find arts and crafts that work for him

Often, when kids are hypersensitive to textures, they miss out on all the cool art projects at school. If your son can't stand anything sticky, slimy, or gooey, then he likely won't be able to engage in any play sessions with Play-Doh or where glue is involved. But if you can find textures that work for him, you can share this knowledge with the school, and that will mean he doesn't miss out.

Here are some simple tips that you may not have thought about before:
- As an alternative for PVA glue, give him a glue stick.
- Offer your son paint markers rather than slimy paint.
- Use sponge-tipped squeeze bottles rather than finger painting or using brushes.
- Try kinetic sand if your son struggles with the scratchy feel of regular sand.
- Provide fidget toys if your son struggles to engage in art lessons at school.

Hypersensitivities can make it difficult for our young sons with ADHD, affecting their lives in more ways than we can count. However, as you can see, there are methods for getting around them; it just takes a little creativity and extra support. Once you find the right strategies for your son, it'll click, and I can't wait for you to watch as the changes take place right in front of you!

Chapter Takeaways

- **Sensory overload and overstimulation are similar, yet different.** Sensory overload is the trigger, while overstimulation is the reaction. Understanding this can be important when talking to others about your son's ADHD.
- **Identify your son's sensory triggers.** By recognizing some of the most common sensory triggers for children with ADHD, including touch, sound, smell, sight, texture, and taste hypersensitivity, you can identify where your son needs support.
- **Overstimulation can have a BIG impact on your son's behavior.** Overstimulation can be incredibly overwhelming, and it's important to recognize how emotional dysregulation like this can impact your son's behaviors, such as becoming irritable, lashing out, or shutting down.
- **Hypersensitivity can affect many aspects of life,** including your son's concentration, stress management, impulse control, and the way he socializes with others.
- **When you recognize your son's triggers, you can help them develop strategies.** By understanding the hypersensitivities out there and learning strategies for these, you can help your son and lessen the effect of overstimulation in his life.
- **Practical support is invaluable for hypersensitivities.** Whether it's weighted blankets for touch hypersensitivity or quiet activities for auditory hypersensitivity, you can offer solutions to your son's hypersensitivity difficulties.

Chapter 4: Navigating the Storm of Your Son's Intense Emotions

"Children are the anchors that hold a mother to life."
— Sophocles

I want to come right out at the start of this chapter and say this: I understand that the concepts of emotional regulation and brain science can be confusing. Due to this, we're not going to get super "sciency" in this chapter. Instead, I want to describe how emotional regulation, or rather dysregulation, works by using a simple example created by Dr. Dan Siegel, a clinical professor of psychiatry and one of the experts I refer to time and time again (Siegel, 2017).

Hold up your hand, fold your thumb into the center of your hand, and close your fingers over your thumb. Your hand represents a brain. Imagine your fingers at the front are where the face is, and your knuckles at the back are the back of the head. Your wrist represents the spinal cord.

When you open your hand back up, your palm represents the first part of the brain to develop, known as the reptilian brain. This part of the brain is responsible for all the vital functions that keep us alive, like our breathing and heart functions. It also helps the rest of the brain communicate with the body by sending messages down the spinal cord.

Now, bend your thumb back into the center of your palm. In this model, your thumb is the limbic area. The limbic area includes the amygdala, which is essentially the emotional hub of the brain—it is where we process all our emotions. It also plays an important role in how we behave in certain situations, particularly those involving our survival and how we respond to stress.

When you fold your fingers over your thumb, your fingers represent the frontal cortex. This part of the brain is one of the last to develop. It oversees processes that help us control our emotions, think critically, have empathy, and tune into others.

So, quick recap: your reptilian brain is the hub for your feelings, while the frontal cortex is the thinking part of your brain.

This is super important to understand when we think about ADHD. Why? you ask me. Well, when we become dysregulated, we essentially "flip our lid". Let's go back to the hand model to explain this—put your hand back in the position to represent a brain, then start hitting your thumb against your fingers. This is what happens when our emotions are overwhelming; our amygdala becomes overactive.

Now, there are only a certain number of hits your fingers (or the frontal cortex) can take before they give up. So, lift your fingers up away from your thumb—this action is what we call "flipping your lid". We flip our lid when we lose control of our emotions—our frontal cortex goes offline, so we're not able to do some of the processes we usually could, like think critically, respond with empathy and understanding, and use our reasoning skills. In this state, we're more likely to react with violence or aggression and lose conscious control of our actions.

Many situations may cause us to flip our lids, and some people are more prone to their lid flipping than others. For example, we're more likely to flip our lid when we're tired or hungry, and we may be more prone to doing it if we have experienced trauma, as this can make our brains more sensitive to stress. Why am I bringing this up? Because children with

ADHD are one of the groups of people that are more likely to flip their lid—here's how.

Get that hand back up and push your thumb against your fingers again. Instead of feeling any resistance, just move your fingers straight up after the first hit. This is what happens in people with ADHD. Recent research looking at the brains of people with ADHD shows that they have an underactive frontal cortex (your fingers) and an overactive amygdala (your thumb) (Herbert, 2023). So, when they feel strong emotions, they find it harder to control. Instead, their emotions take over, and they react using the oldest, most primitive part of their brain. Their frontal cortex goes offline, and they react in ways that they would never dream of doing if their brains weren't overcome with emotions.

Sound familiar? If you're anything like me, you've seen your son flip his lid on at least a bazillion occasions. And, despite what teachers, or even family members who didn't understand, may have said, your son is not choosing to act in this way. He's not acting defiantly, and it's not behavior that needs to be punished or shouted out of him. If his lid gets flipped, he has very little control over what he's doing during this state. Unfortunately for ADHD children, with their slightly different brain structure, becoming emotionally dysregulated like this is more likely to happen.

As their parents, we have to understand this and react accordingly. Here's the thing: I know that's easier said than done. Hey, when Max has hit out at me in the past, or when he went through a period of flipping his lid in the shopping mall almost every time we visited, I lost my cool on more than one occasion. You don't know how to react, right? In that moment, you lose all memory of the tools you've learned to manage this situation, and instead, you simply focus on trying to make the behavior stop in any way you can.

Look, I've been there more times than I can count. That's how I can tell you, with conviction, that you can learn to understand your son's behavior and react differently in these situations. Most importantly, you can look after your son when he flips his lid because, trust me, he doesn't want to be in that state either.

The first step in this tricky journey is knowledge. You need to arm yourself with knowledge about your son and ADHD as a whole before learning to manage his emotions. The first piece of the puzzle you need to think about is your son's emotional intelligence.

Embracing Your Son's Emotional Intelligence

One aspect of ADHD that I haven't discussed yet is how it relates to emotional intelligence. You see, just like with executive functioning, ADHD appears to influence children's emotional intelligence. What is emotional intelligence?

Emotional intelligence (also known as EQ, which stands for "emotional quotient"), is in essence about knowing and being smart about our feelings. It's recognizing how we and others around us feel, and altering our behaviors in accordance with this. EQ includes our ability to identify, display, manage, and use our emotions to communicate with others and relate to them. So, as you can imagine, EQ is vital, as it's important that we can control our emotions to stop us from acting in ways that are considered socially unacceptable.

While most of us usually grow up being taught that IQ is one of the most important skills to have, some experts actually hold emotional intelligence as higher on the ladder of importance, and here's why: new research suggests that our success in life is 80% down to our EQ, while the remaining 20% is due to IQ (Cotruș, Stanciu & Bulborea, 2012; Goleman, 1995). So, what does that mean for our sons with ADHD? And how do ADHD and emotional intelligence relate?

Well, research sheds some light on the relationship between ADHD and EQ. Thomas Brown, PhD (2014), talks about a concept called "emotional flooding", whereby those with ADHD experience intense emotions that overwhelm them, taking up all of their mental space and pushing other feelings and thoughts straight out of their minds. This is like an amygdala hijack, where the most primitive part of the brain takes full control, leading the way to impulsive reactions our sons quickly forget as soon as they calm and the rest of their brain comes back under control (Kristensen et al., 2014). Understanding this dynamic is so vital when trying to support our sons with ADHD, especially when we aim to help them develop their EQ.

Self-regulation and self-awareness are two central components of EQ that our sons with ADHD need to develop to overcome this amygdala hijacking. When we teach them these skills, they learn to manage their emotions in tricky moments and use their EQ to help them. Brown says that people with ADHD can enhance their EQ simply by focusing on the process of identifying and understanding their emotions.

In the next section, I'll give you three evidence-based strategies that have been invaluable for Max and me, and that I truly believe will help you empower your son to build on his EQ. Through doing this, he will learn to identify his emotions, manage these through exercises that actively relax his body, and curb his impulsive behaviors during stressful moments. So, let's get to it!

Teaching Your Son Coping Skills

Helping a son with ADHD to manage his emotions is no walk in the park. You know it, I know it. This isn't because they're resistant to learning, but because their brains are built differently to ours. What's more, they're children, so their brains are naturally less developed than ours.

Often, we'll get told to teach our children feeling words so they can use them when they're dysregulated. Yet identifying feeling words doesn't cut it for children with ADHD, and here's why: ADHD isn't about a lack of emotional knowledge; it's about executive functioning difficulties that cause impulsivity and emotional reactivity. This means that knowing feeling words won't solve the problem. Instead, as parents, we need to focus on teaching our kids three key skills:

1. Normalize his emotions

Children with ADHD experience *normal* emotions. It's totally understandable that they get upset when another kid takes their toy or when they're told to come away from their video games to help us with the laundry. However, the way they feel and respond to those emotions can feel more intense and the emotional outbursts can last longer than they do non-ADHDers because their brains have trouble regulating their emotions.

Teaching your son that his emotions are normal can have a big impact on him, reducing his sense of shame over his emotional reactivity and, as a result, helping him to approach his emotions in a calmer way.

There are a couple of important distinctions to make here:

1. **Normalizing emotions *doesn't* mean downplaying them**: Your son needs to experience and talk about his emotions. Attempting to suppress them will be like trying to keep an inflatable ball underwater—it will always find its way to the surface.
2. **Normalizing emotions *doesn't* mean letting your son react in any way he wants:** Sure, his emotions are normal, but that doesn't mean you need to normalize his behaviors. It's still important to teach him healthy habits for regulating his emotions.

2. Understand what emotions feel like in his body

Just the act of noticing your son's emotions can help him slow down his reactions. Plus, research shows that having a solid understanding of emotions can help children:

1. Calm themselves more quickly.
2. Build stronger friendships.
3. Have fewer negative thoughts.
4. Do better at school.

(ADHD Foundation, 2022)

How can you help your son develop an understanding of emotions? Two of the key strategies to do this is through a) modeling, and b) reflecting. Let's start with modeling.

What I mean by modeling is teaching your son healthy habits by doing them yourself. Studies show that over 80% of parenting is modeling, so let's make use of this when it comes to emotional regulation (Fidelity Charitable, 2023). Start by acknowledging your emotions in front of your son:

- *"Ooh, I'm feeling angry right now. I can feel my body getting hot and tense."*
- *"I can tell I'm feeling sad because my eyes are watering, and my throat feels scratchy."*
- *"I'm feeling anxious right now; my heart is beating fast, and I feel sick."*

Then begin to notice the body signs in your son. For example:

"It looks like you're feeling angry - your hands are balled up into fists."
"You're looking down at the ground - perhaps you're sad."
"You've been struggling to sleep - I struggle to sleep when I'm worried about something."

3. Calming strategies for when he becomes dysregulated

There has been a lot of research into calming strategies for ADHD kids. One of the strategies that consistently comes out on top is mindfulness.

The research looking into the effects of mindfulness on ADHD in children has been pretty promising. For starters, one study found that adolescents with ADHD and their parents (yes, us too!) feel less stressed after a mindfulness program (Bertin, 2023). What's more, mindfulness has been shown to:

- Reduce the intensity of some ADHD symptoms, like impulsivity and emotional reactivity (in this way, mindfulness can help ADHDers learn to regulate their emotions).
- Improve attentional difficulties in children with ADHD.
- Boost their self-esteem.

I already hear your concerns—many kids with ADHD won't be excited by the idea of meditation. In fact, it's hard enough to get adults to meditate, let alone kids. So, here's what I propose and what worked with my son: don't call it "meditation", and make it fun! Here are three of my favorite meditation activities that work great for kids with ADHD:

1. Hot Cocoa Breath: Ages 3 - 7

Start by getting your son to hold up his hands as if he were holding a steaming mug of hot cocoa under his nose. Get him to imagine smelling the hot cocoa. What does it smell like? Does it smell good? Model breathing deeply in through your nose. Then tell him, "It's too hot! It needs to be cooled down!" Model exhaling smoothly over the imaginary surface of the mug through your mouth.

It may take a few times for your son to get it right, but keep it light and fun. Then, when he's feeling dysregulated, you can remind him to smell the hot cocoa.

2. The Breath Button: Ages 3 - 12

The breath button is another simple and easy activity that you can do at home and that you can teach your son to do in school and other settings. You simply choose an object around the house and call it the "breath button". It could be a toy, a special object, or even a piece of furniture or a doorknob.

Every time your child walks past or touches this special object, he has to go and press the breath button. When he does, he takes a big, belly breath, breathing in through his nose and out through his mouth.

This will not only help to calm your son's nervous system, but it will also remind him to be mindful throughout the day.

1. 7/11 Breath: Toddlers to Teens

The technique called 7/11 is super easy to remember, making it a great technique for kids to remind themselves when they need to calm themselves down. They simply need to breathe in for seven seconds and out for eleven. Repeating this a few times will help to calm their nervous systems, reduce the stress they feel, and make them less likely to react impulsively.

Teach your son to repeat 7/11 breaths for 12-15 repetitions, as this will take around 4-6 minutes, which research has shown is enough to improve focus (McGonigal, 2013).

The Pause app is also a great resource for kids, particularly teens, who find it difficult to regulate their emotions and often find solace in their devices.

Whatever you do, remember to be playful with these activities! Your son will have fun if you're having fun. If it becomes a punishment or a chore, he'll be far less likely to do it when he really needs it!

Addressing Comorbid Conditions

When you parent a boy with ADHD, you don't simply parent a boy with ADHD. You parent a boy with ADHD and all of the comorbid conditions that come along with it. What are comorbid conditions? If you're new to the term, "comorbid conditions" (also sometimes called "coexisting conditions") literally means health issues that happen alongside ADHD. The symptoms of comorbid conditions can make it difficult to diagnose and distinguish ADHD, as some of the symptoms may overlap. Unfortunately, all symptoms can sometimes get piled into the ADHD label, which can make it difficult for your son to access other interventions that he needs for his comorbid conditions.

Enough of that negativity—let's learn a little more about ADHD's comorbid conditions, starting with: how common are they?

According to one study, around two-thirds of a sample of 1,919 people with an ADHD diagnosis also had at least one comorbid psychiatric or neurodevelopmental disorder (Reale et al., 2017). For children, learning difficulties are also commonly comorbid with ADHD (Spencer, 2006). However, it appears that fewer children have diagnosed comorbid conditions—research from 2007 found that:

- 33% of children with ADHD had one other comorbid condition
- 16% of children with ADHD had two comorbid conditions
- 18% of children with ADHD had three or more comorbid conditions (I know, that's a lot!)

Now, let's take a look at a full breakdown of the conditions that often coexist with ADHD, starting with the most common:

- **Learning disability:** Approximately 45% of children with ADHD have a learning disability as opposed to 5% of children without ADHD.
- **Conduct disorder:** 27% of children with ADHD are diagnosed with a conduct disorder, in contrast to just 2% in children without ADHD.
- **Anxiety:** 18% of children with, and 2% of children without ADHD have anxiety.
- **Depression:** Only approximately 1% of children who don't have ADHD have diagnosed depression, while 15% of children with ADHD have comorbid depression.

- **Speech problems:** Speech problems are present in 3% of children without ADHD, and 12% of children with ADHD.

(CHADD, 2019)

However, comorbid conditions aren't one size fits all. You remember when I spoke about the different subtypes of ADHD right at the beginning? Well, they come into play here.

We tend to see more cases of oppositional defiance disorder (ODD) in children with combined type ADHD (50.7%) compared to inattentive type (21%) and hyperactive-impulsive type (42%). When it comes to minor depression and generalized anxiety disorder (GAD) though, the figures seem a lot more similar across the board. Minor depression is present in 21% of children with inattentive type *and* hyperactive-impulsive type, and 21.7% in combined type. Of children with inattentive type ADHD and hyperactive-impulsive type ADHD, 19% are diagnosed with GAD, while 12.4% of children with combined type ADHD have GAD (CHADD, 2019).

Finally, there is autism spectrum disorder. Around 30 - 50% of children with ASD display ADHD symptoms, and around 18% of children with ADHD show symptoms of autism (Leitner, 2014). However, the sets of symptoms for the two conditions overlap, so it's common for children to receive a diagnosis for ADHD when it may well be autism, and vice versa.

So, when you're a parent of a child with ADHD, you're managing a lot. If you thought you were just managing the ADHD, you may be sorely mistaken. Of course, with every comorbid condition comes more challenges. The question is: how do you address and manage these?

The first step is to **remember that your son is an individual, not a label**. While this sounds obvious, it's easy to get caught up in the idea of a specific condition, researching the symptoms and best strategies for managing it, without actually thinking about the person: your son. At the end of the day, it doesn't matter what conditions he has, if he's not getting individualized support for these, he won't be able to thrive. So, throw your efforts into developing strategies that work well for him and that can be applied in different settings like in school. This can really help while you're seeking out a diagnosis or waiting for further guidance from your doctor or a mental health professional.

Then, it's important to **take a holistic approach** to your son's care. The term "holistic" simply means focusing on the whole, rather than separate aspects. So, when I talk about "holistic care", I mean looking at all aspects of your son's health, including his social, emotional, and physical needs.

Comorbid conditions can have a big impact on all areas of your son's life, so helping him manage these effects by focusing on his health can put a positive spin on it. Rather than "treating" a condition, he can take care of himself, even treat himself.

Chapter Takeaways

- **Our sons' logical thinking goes offline when they're stressed.** Using Dan Siegel's hand model, we can understand how complex emotional regulation is for our sons with ADHD, and how they can't control their behaviors in moments of stress, but they can learn to.
- **ADHD can make emotional regulation harder.** People with ADHD often experience emotional flooding, effectively hijacking the amygdala and making it overactive, causing impulsive behaviors and a loss of control.
- **Emotional intelligence is so important for our sons to master.** Emotional intelligence is important for all of us, but especially our sons with ADHD. Mastering EQ helps our sons to understand, identify, and manage their emotions, which can help them navigate stressful situations.

- **Self-awareness and self-regulation are the key to success.** Teaching our sons self-awareness and self-regulation around their emotions can help them identify and manage these effectively.
- **It's not enough to face ADHD head on, we also need to consider comorbid conditions.** Our sons with ADHD will likely experience comorbid conditions, such as anxiety, depression, or learning difficulties. We need to approach our sons' ADHD with a holistic care point of view, tailoring our support to their needs.

* * *

And now for your next two bonus toolkits…

Firstly, the **ADHD Behavior Tracker,** which is a practical tool for tracking daily goals, medication, and behavior, designed to help boys with ADHD monitor their progress and manage their symptoms effectively.

Secondly, you have the **Anger Management Toolkit for Kids,** which is an extensive set of resources including a calendar, planner, anger control tips, and tracking tools to help boys with ADHD understand and manage their anger effectively.

Just scan the QR code below to access the toolkits!

Chapter 5: Boosting Your Son's Executive Function & Problem-Solving Skills

"A child can teach an adult three things: to be happy for no reason, to always be curious, and to fight tirelessly for something."
– Paulo Coelho

Guess what? You're halfway through the book. Woohoo! In this chapter, I'll be delving right into the world of executive function and problem-solving in ADHD. I've already covered executive function in our sons with ADHD in one sense, but that was only so you can understand how ADHD and executive functioning go hand in hand. This chapter, however, is packed *full* of practical strategies. So, I'll be taking what we know about executive functioning and ADHD and translating it into techniques to help you support your son to develop his:

- Planning & organizational skills
- Focus, attention, and working memory
- Problem-solving skills

I'll also cover how you can parent in a way that encourages your son's independence *and* embraces his mistakes, so he can see them as learning opportunities, not disasters.

First, let's have a quick recap on executive functions, because it was over four chapters ago, so it's okay if your memory of it is a little rusty. Executive functions are a vital set of skills in our brain's management system. We need these skills to do things like plan, set goals, and executive tasks, which we must be able to do during daily life.

More and more research links ADHD with problems with executive function, like that study we talked about in the intro showing that 89% of children with ADHD struggle with at least one area of executive functioning.

Problem-solving is one part of executive function that hasn't got much of mention yet. That doesn't mean to say that it's not important—quite the opposite, in fact. Let me paint you a picture with another story about Max.

When Max was four, he got given a whack-a-mole-type game. I wanted to let him try to figure out how it worked first before intervening, as I was trying to encourage his independence at the time. As I watched him try to figure out what was going on and how to play the game, he became increasingly more distressed, until he picked up the game and was about to throw it. As you can imagine, at that point, I intervened.

We had this same issue when it came to homework. This happened frequently, but I can particularly remember a time when he was six. He was tasked to complete some math homework, but math isn't his strongest subject. I could see him trying to figure out what he needed to do, but he just couldn't get to grips with it. Well, after about ten minutes of not understanding it, he shredded the homework completely. It wasn't enough to just rip it in two, he proceeded to shred it into teeny, tiny pieces. Bye bye, homework!

If you've struggled with similar situations with your son, I feel your pain! It can be so difficult to watch them become distraught because they find problem-solving so hard. Once I found ways to help Max, I felt a lot less helpless in those situations and, more importantly, helped *him* feel far more in control. So, let's move on to the strategies, shall we? We'll start with planning and organization.

Developing Your Son's Planning & Organizational Skills

Planning and organizational skills are invaluable—they're like our roadmap, helping us navigate daily life. They not only help us anticipate what lies ahead of us, but also decide the path we're going to take and the way we'll tackle different tasks and hurdles that crop up along the way. For our sons with ADHD, who struggle with executive functions like this, planning and organization can feel elusive.

As a fellow parent of a son with ADHD, you'll know the struggles with your son's lack of organization and planning. A prime example is the dreaded morning rush. When Max was in elementary school, trying to entice him to get ready in the morning was a literal nightmare. Tasks that I felt were so simple, like dressing or getting his school bag ready, turned into full-on arguments, yelling, tantrums, and tears. There was one morning I'll never forget (involving homework again, dreaded homework!)—Max and I had spent two hours the night before completing his homework, only for him to leave it on the kitchen table the next morning.

I noticed it after he'd already left for the bus. So, I gave him a call, and he ran back to get it. He stuffed his homework into his bag, seemingly not considering that it needed to be in one piece when he gave it to his teacher. Throughout the distraction, he forgot his coat. After he'd left the house and come back twice for things he'd forgotten, the school bus arrived and he missed it. The stress and tension that morning as I was driving him to school (me now late for work and him late for school), was a time I won't soon forget.

Situations like this show us how vital planning and organization are. However, there are other, arguably more important, roles for these skills. For example, research consistently shows that planning and organization link to academic achievement and how well we interact with others in social settings. What's more, planning and organizational skills are important for our overall well-being, as children who struggle with these skills typically experience more stress (mine and Max's morning rushes are certainly a testament to this!), lower confidence levels, and continual difficulties meeting what is expected of them, both at home and in other settings, which can cause a steep decline in their self-esteem.

This has sounded pretty gloomy so far, hasn't it? That's not my intent—I know you'll understand the harsh realities of the impact ADHD can have on your son's organization and planning. Here's the bright side: just like anything, with the right support and guidance, your son can significantly improve his planning and organizational abilities. It'll take practice and determination from both of you, but trust me, it's doable.

After speaking with many parents of children with ADHD, I know that I speak for them when I say that visual aids are a *lifesaver*. These practical tools help our sons with ADHD stay on track and reduce distractions. Let's go through some of the most effective visual aids to help develop your son's planning and organizational skills.

The first pieces of the planning and organizational puzzle are checklists. These tools offer structure and organization, which can be extremely helpful for our sons with ADHD who struggle to stay organized and plan ahead. Checklists help by breaking down bigger tasks into small, more manageable chunks, which can help our sons feel less overwhelmed and organize their actions. Research shows that this supports children with ADHD to complete tasks like their homework and reduce forgetfulness (Langberg et al., 2010).

The next visual aid that it's vital to have at your disposal is a visual timetable. Visual timetables also aid our sons, as they make the day feel predictable and create a routine which reduces any anxiety around unexpected changes. It also means they're not stuck not knowing what's going to happen throughout the day.

Research shows that visual timetables help to improve their independence, which can make them feel more in control and reduce tantrums and other difficult behaviors (Thomas & Karuppali, 2022).

Other visual aids that are worth having in your arsenal (and recommending to your son's teachers) are graphs, charts, and illustrations. Graphs—rather than a mix of confusing words—help our children to immediately understand the pattern of a relationship between two factors; this clear presentation of data can help them understand complex information.

Charts, like mind maps and flowcharts, also help to break down difficult information, making it organized and thus the main points easier to understand. And then there are illustrations, which are much easier for visual learners, including many kids with ADHD, to understand. Illustrations tend to stick in their memory better (and also make learning more fun!).

Strengthening His Focus, Attention, and Working Memory

Strengthening your son's focus will do wonders for him in the classroom setting, but also at home when he needs to settle slightly or complete a task like get ready for school or doing his homework. As we know, focus, attention, and working memory are affected by ADHD, making tasks involving these executive functions more difficult.

Fortunately, there are strategies to help your son boost his focus, attention, and working memory. They include the following.

1. Creating a structured environment (where possible)

Creating a structured environment works for some tasks, but not so much for others. For example, you can create a workspace where your son can do homework that has minimal distractions and encourages him to focus, like keeping the walls near his desk blank, removing all objects that he might get distracted by, and turning off the TV and other screens.

Creating a structured environment is also crucial for your son's working memory, and the reason for this is the "congruency effect". So, when you're trying to remember something, being distracted can take the brain power away from working memory, meaning that the information your son is processing effectively falls on deaf ears—it doesn't go in and get processed properly (Lorenc, Mallett & Lewis-Peacock, 2021).

2. Understand and practice focus

When considering focus and attention, it's important that you and your son are on the same page. For example, saying "Pay attention!" when your son gets distracted during a task likely won't sink in. Why? Well, because he *is* paying attention, just not to the task you want him to. This may mean that your son shouts back "I *am* paying attention" because he is.

So, when getting your son to focus on a task like homework or a chore, it's important to get specific. Say, "Hey, let's refocus on your homework, shall we?" or "Max—pay attention to what I'm showing you on the washer."

And like any skills in life, focusing and paying attention take practice. So, if you want your son to improve these abilities, treat attention like an endurance skill—start slow and for short periods, then gradually increase it as you would a run. However, kids with ADHD need time for their mind to wander, too, so ensure you include lots of breaks.

Other helpful strategies that I've already covered are:
- **Mindfulness meditation:** This helps to quiet our sons' minds, making it easier for them to stay focused and pay attention to the task at hand.
- **Being physically active:** Physical exertion right before your son needs to focus on a task that uses working memory will help, as it will reduce his hyperactivity and allow him to sit still for longer times. If your son struggles to sit still through a task, plop a sensory break (where he can go and run around) right smack-bang in the middle of the task, allowing him to let off some steam and then return to the task.

Teaching Your Son How to Problem-Solve

Problem-solving is another key skill that falls under the bracket of executive functions, making it infinitely tricky for our sons with ADHD. While problem-solving may not come naturally to our sons (and, in fact, may feel like an impossible hill to climb), it is possible for them to learn how to problem solve. It just takes some extra time spent practicing.

The best way to teach your son how to problem-solve is by incorporating it into your everyday lives. There are many opportunities for you to encourage your son to problem-solve throughout the day. Let's consider some scenarios:

- **When something doesn't go to plan:** If a plan goes awry or you face sudden changes, you can say, "Oh. That didn't quite go to plan, did it? Shall we think of ways to get back on track?" or "What do you think would be the best thing to do next?"
- **Playing games:** Problem-solving games like Sudoku, crosswords, and board games get your son to analyze and consider multiple

options as well as implement strategy and cunning. While playing these games, you can encourage your son to problem-solve by saying, "Ooh, what are you going to do next?" or "That bit looks tricky— how are you going to do it?"

- **Your morning routine:** As a parent, it has always amazed me how many things can go wrong during the morning routine. Shoes are never where you need them to be, you unexpectedly run out of cereal, your son forgets his lunch. On and on and on the problems go. You can reduce this by encouraging your son to problem-solve; for example, the night before, you can say, "Right, what could you do now to make your life easier tomorrow morning?" or "Tomorrow morning you'll wake up and need to get dressed, get your bag and shoes, and eat breakfast. What could you do now that future you will thank you for?"

OK, now let's get to the specifics on what strategies you can use to really help your son develop his problem-solving skills. I present: The Problem-Solving Wheel.

The Problem-Solving Wheel works like this: you create a wheel with a problem in the middle. For example, "I'm struggling to focus on the task." Then, around the middle, write all of the possible solutions for the problem. In this scenario, it may be:

- Run around the garden for five minutes.
- Have a quick break and eat a fruit snack.
- Remove three distractions from my workspace.
- Put my headphones on to block out noise.
- Take a ten-minute break and come back.

This guides your son through problem-solving without needing to say anything. You can just prompt him to look at his problem-solving wheel, and he can decide the solution that would work best.

Another tool that Max and I *love* is a simple mind map (or a "brainstorm bubble" as we call it). This works similarly to the problem-solving wheel, but you can get a little more creative with it. If your son is into any particular games or shows, you can use his favorite character and go nuts with this one.

For example, "Bluey keeps getting frustrated and hitting her brother." This could go into the bubble in the middle of the page. Then, with arrows coming off, ask your son, "What could Bluey do in this situation that might help her?" This could be:

- Take a few deep breaths.
- Imagine being in a relaxing place.
- Tense her muscles and then relax them.
- Go for a walk.
- Wrap herself in a comforting blanket.
- Write down what's upsetting her.

And so on. I recommend completing this brainstorm bubble when your son is calm, and then coming back to it in the moments he needs it. What I love about this strategy is all you have to say, "Let's look at what Bluey might do in this situation" then "Which one do you think Bluey might like right now?"

For older kids, you don't have to center your brainstorm bubble around a character—it all depends on your child's development level! Just give it a go and see what happens. For practicing problem-solving in another super-fun yet slightly more mature way, here are some games that test those problem-solving brain cells:

Board games:
- Guess Who
- Clue
- Connect 4

- iTrax
- Tic Tac Toe
- Chess
- Scrabble
- Sudoku

Video games:
- Minecraft
- The Legend of Zelda series
- Portal

Parenting in a Way That Encourages Independence

Our sons have so many wacky and wonderful ideas—perhaps they've come up with an idea for the best way to get ready in the morning, or how to focus in the best way possible. Whatever it is, as parents, we want to encourage and respect these ideas, as they help our sons become more independent. This is so important for any child with an additional need, as the narrative they're often told in schools and the stigma is that they aren't as able to do things independently. When others believe this, they start to automatically limit their expectations of our sons, which communicates to our sons that they're not capable of being independent.

Unfortunately, this can result in what is known as "learned helplessness". The first studies on this were done with animals, so I'll use this analogy to describe what it means. In 1967, professors Seligman and Maier exposed dogs to a series of electric shocks (horrible, I know) (Leonard, 2023). One set of dogs couldn't control the electric shocks, so they would come at completely random times. The second set of dogs could press a level to stop the electric shocks.

In a follow-up study, the first set of dogs was able to avoid the electric shocks by jumping over a barrier. However, they didn't attempt to escape, thinking that they had no control. They had learned to become helpless (Maier & Seligman, 2016).

It's the same with our sons (although less awful, thankfully). When our sons are repeatedly taught that they can't be independent or that they need others' help, they begin to believe that for everything they do. So, as parents, we need to encourage our sons' independence, as this will help them become autonomous as they grow and become adults.

How can you parent your son in a way that encourages his independence? Well, you can **start by thinking of your son's independence as a triangle.** At the bottom of the triangle is the green zone, representing all the tasks your son can do perfectly well on his own. He's got those things locked down.

Then, in the middle of the triangle is the orange zone. This is the 50/50 zone comprised of the tasks that your son can do independently half of the time, but needs assistance with the other half of the time. Whether he can do them independently or not may alter based on his mood, the time of day and when he takes his medication, where he is, and so on.

Finally, you have the top of the triangle: the red zone, called "My Ultimate Goals". These are the tasks that your son can't do independently right now, but he would like to be able to do in the future.

As your son works on tasks within the orange zone, he will become more confident at these. When he's doing these tasks independently all of the time, he can move to the green zone tasks. Then he can pull a goal down from the red zone and place it in the orange zone and start working on being more independent with this task.

You can talk your son through this and have it as a visual in the home where tasks are placed on with Velcro so that he can move them to different positions. By doing this, you create a line of open communication and it works much like a reward or a target—it feels rewarding to be able to move the tasks down the triangle into the green zone.

Secondly, to improve your son's independence, you need to identify how you can handle the discomfort of letting your son fall down, make mistakes, and learn from these - this is what I'll cover next.

Embracing Your Son's Mistakes, and Teaching Him to Do the Same

Ever found yourself exhausted by the threats that seem to be all around your son? A sharp corner here, a steep step there, a hazard that seems like it's bound to cause an injury. Witnessing Max stumble and fall is something I have always found incredibly tough as a mom. And there's a good reason for this—as parents, we are literally hardwired to want to protect our children at all costs. They rely on us for survival and to teach them how to navigate the world. When you're a parent of a son with ADHD, this feeling is even more heightened, because these sons seem even more vulnerable.

Children with ADHD naturally face more obstacles and mistakes because of their unique cognitive makeup, so learning how to manage when they make errors and coming back from these all guns blazing, rather than defeated, is a vital part of life, and a skill we, as parents, need to teach.

Research shows that encouraging children with ADHD to have a growth mindset not only boosts their academic performance, but can also increase their motivation and make it easier for them to get along with peers and make friends (Rattan et al., 2015).

It isn't easy though, is it? First, we may be more nervous due to our children's vulnerability and want to protect and shelter them from life's difficulties. Secondly, when our kids with ADHD face setbacks, they may be more likely to experience feelings of inadequacy or self-doubt, because they have dealt with so many such obstacles.

The best way to counteract fears of making mistakes and failure is for you to think in terms of "good enough" rather than "perfect" and model this to your son. What I mean by this is recognizing that no one is ever perfect, and that perfect is unattainable. However, with mistakes and errors, you learn to grow and be "good enough" at something.

Start this by normalizing mistakes. Encourage your son to have an accepting attitude toward his mistakes by showing him that mistakes are just a natural part of the learning process. For example, take your son to try a skill he hasn't done before, like rock climbing. Get him to watch you before he starts, and verbalize the mistakes as you make them. For example, "Right, I'm going to put my foot up here. Oops, that wasn't the right spot and it meant I couldn't keep my grip so I fell. Ah well, time to try again."

By modeling yourself making mistakes in life and being accepting of these, you can teach your son to do the same. If you keep consistent with it, before you know it, you'll hear your son say, "Oh no, I did that wrong. Let me try it this way." And when that moment comes, let me tell you, you'll be a proud parent indeed!

Then, **add in praise for effort and progress.** We've got into a bad habit in our society of offering praise for results (product) and not for effort (process). So rather than focusing on your son's test results (product: score of 9/10) you need to celebrate his effort. If you can see he's working really hard at a task, say, "Wow, you worked so hard there. Good job" or "Look at the progress you made! That's amazing." This not only spurs your son to continue working hard but it also encourages a growth mindset, which will help him overcome his mistakes.

Chapter Takeaways

- **Boys with ADHD struggle with executive function.** So, they need a little more support than neurotypical kids with activities that involve planning, organization, focusing, paying attention, problem solving, and so on.
- **Visual aids are a lifesaver for planning and organization.** Visual aids like visual timetables and checklists work wonders for supporting ADHD boys' planning and organizational skills.
- **Create a structured environment to support your son's focus, attention, and working memory.** If your son is surrounded by distractions, he's going to struggle to concentrate. So, remove distractions and incorporate physical activity and mindfulness to calm his body and mind.
- **There are opportunities to practice problem-solving everywhere.** Including problem-solving opportunities in everyday activities, as well as using fun tools like the Problem-Solving Wheel and brainstorm bubbles can help your son develop his ability to problem solve.
- **Encourage your son's independence.** Use the Independence Triangle and encourage your son to develop a "good enough" mindset so that he doesn't feel downhearted when he inevitably makes mistakes.

Chapter 6: Setting Your Son Up for Life with Healthy Habits

"Children are not things to be molded, but are people to be unfolded."
– Jess Lair

When parenting a son with ADHD, there's one thing you will be *constantly* bombarded with: advice on how best to raise him—cue the internal eye role. The advice starts with what they should be eating, and often includes how you should "discipline" them. The list goes on without end.

When Max and I were first navigating his diagnosis, I was receiving advice (mostly unsolicited, by the way) left, right, and center. To be honest, it felt downright overwhelming, because I wanted to do right by my son. All parents want to get it right so their children can thrive. However, more often than not, I felt like I was getting it wrong, and this was never truer than at bedtime.

Picture this: it's late and your son just won't get to sleep. You've been trying for a good hour now to get him to settle, but he's still bouncing off the walls. He's a big ol' ball of energy. You try everything: stories, an audiobook, calming music, and even a forty-five-minute car journey to get him to sleep. Still, nothing. He's wide awake, thoughts racing and mind wandering. That's about how it was for a good two years with Max.

He got to age seven and I was at the end of my tether. I'd tried sleeping aids, melatonin, and all that jazz, but none of it seemed to touch Max; he just could not settle. I was on the verge of losing my mind as I was so tired, and so was poor Max. His teachers said he was tired at school, and this only made his behavior worse. I had to find strategies that worked, and I needed to find them fast.

That's when I reached out to a clinical psychologist to give me advice or *anything* that would get Max off to sleep (and me in bed at a reasonable time!). Want to know their main guidance? Setting a consistent sleep schedule. It also involved other healthy habits, including nutrition, exercise, and limiting screen time, that help kids with ADHD in so many ways.

In this chapter, I'll share this advice and give you strategies to instill healthy habits in your son, not just around sleep, but also for everything he's doing. Before you know it, your son will be sleeping soundly each and every night and forming healthy life habits without the to-ing and fro-ing that may be plaguing your life right now.

The Power of the Almighty Sleep Schedule

Sleep is a necessity for all of us. While we sleep, our bodies work to support our brains, ensuring we're physically *and* mentally healthy and rested. In children and teens, sleep is also a time when they can grow, develop, and repair after days spent running around.

Not getting enough sleep can have many detrimental effects. Of course, lack of sleep makes us feel tired, which makes everything so much more difficult, but it can also increase our risk of chronic health problems, and alter how we think, learn, react, and get along in social situations. Consistently not getting enough sleep has many, many other physiological effects, too, but I won't bore you by going into a full-blown "sciencey" explanation about them. Just know that sleep is incredibly important for us.

Yet, despite our best attempts at getting our sons to sleep, bedtime often becomes a battle: you vs. ADHD body and brain. It's like Jiu Jitsu: you're trying your best to fight against it, but only to subdue rather than to injure. Unfortunately, ADHD can be like an unhinged opponent, and it ends up being more like a bull fight than a civilized Jiu Jitsu match.

Bedtimes is also one of the areas that we as parents receive the *most* unsolicited advice. I mean, why do people feel the need? Let me lay out *exactly* what the clinical psychologist suggested.

1. **Calming bedtime routine**

Having a consistent calming bedtime routine helps our circadian rhythms know that it's time to sleep, meaning it's easier to drift off when our heads actually hit the pillow.

Calming bedtime routines are vital for kids with ADHD, as they need time to unwind and relax their minds before trying to drift off. So, ensure your son starts his routine an hour or even an hour and a half before bedtime.

So, it's all well and good telling you to create a bedtime routine, but what should you include in it? Here is what the clinical psychologist recommended:

- **Evening exercise:** Now, not many people would include evening sprints or exercise in a calming bedtime routine. However, quick, intense exercise can be so handy when you're trying to get your son to settle, especially if hyperactivity is to blame for the insomnia.

- **Bath with Epsom Salt/Magnesium Sulfate:** Magnesium is a natural mineral that many parents claim can work well for kids with ADHD as it helps to calm them down, lessening hyperactivity, impulsivity, *and* inattentiveness. However, it's important to note that the research into this was done in the late 1990s, and the study was pretty weak, and nothing has been shown since. Therefore, it's important to take this with a pinch of (Epsom) salt (Newmark, 2021).
- **Reading in bed:** This bedtime activity works well for some, but not for others, so there may be some trial and error here. Some kiddos with ADHD will find reading before bed super soothing, while others won't at all. Max needs a book he's gripped by to actually read it, but then that stops him from sleeping, so it was a no-no in our house. That isn't to say it won't work for your son!
- **Yoga sleep exercises:** Yoga provides the best of both worlds: it's relaxing *and* it's a form of exercise, making it perfect for our ADHD kids that need to release some energy before bedtime. Yoga can also boost our sons' confidence and increase their mental and physical discipline over time. The knack is to try and make it fun.

2. Setting a realistic regular bedtime

Consistency is well and truly the key when it comes to bedtime for kids with ADHD. Establishing a regular bedtime routine and then going to bed at the same time each night will help to regulate your son's internal clock and encourage a more restful night's sleep.

However, I know from experience how tricky it can be to keep this up, especially on weekends! One of the issues that many parents with kids with ADHD have is that they set *unrealistic* bedtimes. Our kids are going to lie awake if they go to bed too early, and this will only serve to make them frustrated and anxious, and they'll likely end up in our beds or disturbing our sacred time of peace! So, find a bedtime that works well for your son and stick to it with a vengeance.

3. Waking up at the same time, each day (even weekends)

Waking up at the same time each day is just as important as getting a regular bedtime. Letting him lie in on a Friday or Saturday while you do the dishes and laundry may sound a lot easier than multitasking, but it's in the best interest of your son's sleep that he gets up at the same time each day. Sacrifice an hour on the weekend for perhaps one, two, or even three extra hours each night while your son sleeps peacefully—I'll take that!

4. Keeping his bedroom cool, quiet, and dark

Creating a sleep environment that oozes relaxation is a vital part of healthy sleep habits for our ADHD kids, and part of this is making sure it's cool, quiet, and dark. Temperature plays an important role in sleep quality as we tend to get a better night's sleep in a cooler room, as this helps our natural body temperature to drop, which typically happens when we're in the early stages of falling asleep (Pacheco & Rosen, 2024). The ideal temperature is 65-68°F.

What's more, blocking out unwanted light and creating a dark bedroom space is highly conducive to sleep for our energetic kids, as it helps their brains identify that it's nighttime, and therefore time to sleep. For added darkness, consider getting your son an eye mask, as this can block out any residual light creeping in.

Here are some other strategies that parents of kids with ADHD swear by:

- Weighted blanket
- Audiobooks/podcasts
- Lavender diffuser

These all promote relaxation and make for an awesome bedtime routine. However, just be aware that all children are different, so what works for one may not work for the other.

Nutrition and Exercise: The Healthy Habit Essentials

I touched on diet and exercise a little bit in Chapter 1, when I spoke about non-traditional treatment methods, but it's not surprising they're cropping back up. Getting the right nutrition and amount of exercise is, of course, essential for your son's physical health, but time and time again research has shown it also has many positive effects on ADHD symptoms. We already know the ins and outs of *why* we should get our kids to eat well and exercise regularly, so now, let's talk about *how* we get them to do this.

When trying to implement healthy eating and regular exercise habits with Max, I didn't really know where to begin, so I went to what I often turn to: books. Specifically, James Clear's *Atomic Habits*. I used his guidance and applied these to nutrition and exercise habits with my son, and it worked a treat. Here are the key things that made a difference:

1. **Start small**

Your son is never going to take to a new, healthy habit if it comes with big, sudden changes. So, start small. Pick a small element of the healthy habit, like adding one healthy food or physical activity, and mix that in with your son's weekly routine. For example, if he has pizza once a week, add a vegetable on top. If your son's fussy with veggies, you can get creative: make a game out of him trying a new food, or even a reward system where he works towards a reward he really wants.

2. **Make it obvious**

Clear states in his book that we tend to choose healthy habits if they're obvious, and we're less likely to choose unhealthy habits if they're not visible and obvious. So, keep healthy foods in places that are highly visible and accessible in your home. For example, put a fruit bowl down in the lounge or a nutritious snack box on the counter. Place it in plain sight, and make sugary snack foods harder to find.

3. **Set goals around exercise and nutrition**

If your son works well with goals, brainstorm some specific, achievable goals relating to eating and exercise. Examples of this could be:

- To eat at least one serving of fruit or veg with every meal.
- To only eat sugary snacks and drinks once or twice a week.
- Do a form of exercise for at least thirty minutes every day.
- Walk 10,000 steps each day.

Making these small, slight changes in your son's routine can have a big impact on his overall health, and you'll likely see changes in his ADHD symptoms, too. However, there is one healthy habit that many parents have searched and searched for the answer to and haven't yet found—how to limit their son's screen time. So, we'll tackle this one next. Buckle up!

Say "No" to Endless Screen Time

This is a controversial topic among parents with kids with ADHD, but I'm going to broach it as it's an important one. And let me start with this: a large study from 2019 examining the effects of screen-time in preschoolers found that children who had more than two hours per day of screen time were 7.7 times more likely to meet the diagnostic criteria for ADHD. It seems particularly linked to inattention; as screen time goes up, so do problems with inattention in preschoolers (Tamana et al., 2019). Furthermore, a meta-analysis from 2023 found a significant relationship between excessive screen exposure and ADHD (Liu et al., 2023).

But let's get one thing straight. I am in no way saying that any child wouldn't have ADHD if they weren't exposed to screens. I'm also not saying that ADHD is the only factor increasing the risk of ADHD in kids. There are many, many factors that all play a part; it's a complex condition. Yet the research is interesting, isn't it? The World Health Organization also recommends no screen time for one-year-olds and less than an hour in one sitting for two-year-olds, so it's important to keep this in mind when we're exposing our kids to screens.

However, I *know* how tough it is in our modern world. Screens are such a temptation, both for us and the kids. As I've said 100 times already, parenting is hard work. Juggling work, the endless to-do list of household chores, and just the general tasks of daily life, sometimes we desperately crave a moment of peace and quiet. Most parents in our modern world would say that screen time offers just that: a moment of respite.

So, whether it's a quick episode of "Bluey" to calm an oncoming tantrum or ten minutes of "Paw Patrol" while we cook dinner, screens have a lot of pluses for us parents. But, and it's a huge but, we can't ignore the evidence of the consequences that screen time can have on our kids, particularly on our sons with ADHD.

The question is: what are we to do? It's a tricky balance, a parenting tightrope walk, especially if you haven't put screen-time boundaries in place from the outset, but this is what you can do to reduce your son's screen time:

1. **Step away from *your* screens**

Our kids are keen observers, so what we do, our kids follow. If you spend extended periods on your phone or laptop, your son is going to pick up on this and assume that's what we do with devices.

Setting boundaries around screen time starts with modeling the behavior you want to see in your son. Make a conscious effort to put your phone any other screens away during family time, particularly with mealtimes and playtime, as well as bedtime stories. Always prioritize face-to-face time over screens.

And remember this when you next whip your phone out in front of your son: you're not just setting the rules for your son but you're also shaping his attitude and behavior towards technology for many, many years to come.

2. Prioritize tech-free time

It's our job as parents to carve out time in our family's busy schedule for tech-free time. Whether it's going to the park together as a family, having a board game night, or just spending some time outside in the garden, quality time is important for our sons with ADHD.

What I mean by prioritizing tech-free time is: make it fun. The reason why our sons love screens is because they're entertaining—they provide instant rewards and keep them engaged. So, let's aim to do that in our tech-free time, too. Plan fun activities that will keep them interested, and you may just find they don't gravitate towards screens during this time.

3. Set the boundary then validate, validate, validate

Unfortunately, setting the boundary is only half of the battle. The other half, the real war, is managing our children's difficult responses with empathy and understanding. Like us adults, children want to feel like they're heard and understood, especially when they're mad at us for taking their screen time away. So, when you set a boundary around screen time, make sure you validate your son's emotions and perspectives.

Start by clearly communicating the boundary and the reasons why you're doing this—not in a harsh or judgmental way, but in a way that shows him that you understand that he loves his screen, but it's important for his health that there are limits. For example, "In our family, we only spend two hours a day on our screens, because this is what is recommended for our health."

Then, come in with the validation. "I know it's tough because you really love watching your show. I get it." And after validating, reinforce the boundary and offer a choice. For example, "We only have two hours a day of screen time. What would you like to do instead—coloring or play together outside?"

Remember, boundary setting and validation aren't one-time things. It's an ongoing process, and it will be particularly difficult at the beginning, as you're only just starting to make the change. Be prepared to reinforce your boundary over and over again, while offering empathy and understanding for how your son feels.

If you stay consistent and offer empathy, your son will know what to expect, and feel seen and heard. And while he may not like your boundary, he will eventually follow it.

Chapter Takeaways

- **Sleep is a vital healthy habit our sons need to lock down.** It's fundamental for physical *and* mental health for our sons, as it supports their cognitive function, emotional regulation, and general well-being.
- **Bedtimes are *hard* with a child with ADHD.** Yet, you can learn to manage this so it doesn't become a battle. Establishing a consistent bedtime routine and conducive sleep environment that's tailored to your son's needs can provide the structure and relaxation he needs for a successful night's sleep.

- **Nutrition and exercise can fuel the ADHD brain.** These healthy lifestyle habits are linked to better well-being in our children and a reduction in ADHD symptoms. So, start small, make the healthy food choices visible, and set achievable goals.
- **Reducing screen time is tricky, but not impossible.** Evidence repeatedly shows that screen time can negatively influence ADHD symptoms. By modeling healthy device habits, coming up with fun alternative activities, and validating our sons' emotions when setting boundaries, we can strike the right balance and keep our boundaries consistent.
- **Setting boundaries is about more than just rules.** It's about providing a structure around screen time while offering empathy and understanding so our sons feel seen and heard, and that their views and feelings are appreciated.

* * *

To help reenforce those healthy habits, just scan the QR code below to unlock your fourth bonus toolkit, the **ADHD Mental Health Bundle.**

This bundle is a comprehensive set of tools including breathing techniques, anxiety trackers, goal setting, daily journals, and mindfulness exercises designed to help boys with ADHD manage anxiety, set and achieve goals, and maintain overall mental health.

Chapter 7: Helping Your Son Build Positive Relationships

> *"The potential possibilities of any child are the most intriguing and stimulating in all creation."*
> – Ray L. Wilbur

I'm no relationship expert but, as a mental health expert specializing in ADHD and a mom of an ADHD son, I have learned a thing or two about the challenges our sons have or are likely to face with relationships, not just with their peers and their siblings, but also with us.

Let's face it, while our sons are the light of our lives, and their ADHD brings many incredible qualities, there's no denying that ADHD can create some pretty choppy waters, especially as you try to figure out how best to support them. During that time, your bond can take a bit of a hit. And if your relationship is taking hit after hit, and you're the most patient with your son of anyone, what is it like for your son with others, such as his teachers and siblings, who don't understand him as well as you do?

Evidence tells us that children with ADHD typically struggle to understand social cues, make strong friendships, and keep their emotions under control during arguments and fall outs (Chronis et al., 2004). They also tend to have more difficult relationships with their siblings (Mikami & Pfiffner, 2008).

So, it's safe to say that times can get tough when it comes to our sons and relationships. When these times come (if they haven't come for you already), it's good to know how to manage. So, in this chapter, I'll focus on how you can strengthen your bond with your son and manage the stresses that can arise between an ADHD boy and his siblings, and how you can help your son through peer relationships problems.

Strengthening Your Bond with Your Son

My relationship with Max is good now but, let me tell you, it wasn't always like this. There was one point where I had had enough. It was when he was six years old and I felt like I was drowning. I kept getting calls from school about him not listening and generally being a hyperactive ADHD kid, and we were butting heads so much at home that I thought I was going to lose my mind.

If this resonates with you, and you're desperately trying to find a way to strengthen the bond with your son, you're not alone. Many parents of kids with ADHD have this same issue. In fact, a parent on Reddit said, "I really love my child, he is the light of my life, he makes me laugh every day, and he is a treasure. All of that is true, but at the same time I am so tired of parenting an ADHD child and I just can't find the support I need."
(FacelessOldWoman1234, 2021).

The problem we get with being their closest person is that we're also the one that gets the brunt of their behaviors. It's like a love/hate relationship. This means that it's common to "fall out" with your son often, as you battle against one another, with him getting angry at you, and you getting angry right back! Unfortunately, this comes with a whole load of parental guilt. All parents want to feel close to their kids, and let's be honest, it sucks when we feel a rift form. And our kids feel it too, and this shows in how responsive they are to us. Research shows that a child is more likely to follow their parent's directions if they have a strong bond with them. If there is a breakdown in the relationship, will they listen to you? It's unlikely. For both of these reasons, it's important to learn ways to strengthen your bond with your son.

So, how do you go about keeping that relationship strong with your son, even when it keeps taking a beating? It's about making small changes to how you navigate the everyday. These small changes have a big, big impact.

1. Take time out to play with your son

Whatever age your son is, he wants to spend time with you. If your son is of playing age, say yes when he invites you to play with him. It doesn't matter what it is: building blocks, dress-up, riding bikes. The main point of playing together is spending quality time together and laughing whenever possible. When you laugh together, this stimulates the release of endorphins, so-called "happy hormones" which make you both feel more connected and loved.

If your son is older, he may not be so enticed by play. If he is a teen and you suggested playing with building blocks, he'd likely roll his eyes at you and perhaps ignore you completely! That doesn't mean you can't play with him—if he's into video games, ask to join. Or if he has other interests, ask if he can teach you. Just showing an interest in his interests offers you an opportunity to bond.

2. Make the most of small moments

Each day is made up of the sum of its parts: the small moments that we have with our kids. These moments, when combined, can make a big impact on how we feel about ourselves and how connected we feel to others.

I noticed this when I started to make small changes. When Max was in elementary school, I used to wake him up by saying, "Come on, it's time to get up!" with a kiss on the forehead. We'd proceed to get ready for the day, and it was as if I'd woken up grumpy at him—I'd be short with him and lose my composure easily. I think part of me woke up dreading the school rush, and it showed. We'd leave the house having barely said a word to one another other than for practical purposes, and he'd go off to school without a single moment of connection.

When learning about the power of small moments, I decided to make some minute changes. When I woke Max up, I'd go in five minutes before he needed to get up and I'd give him a snuggle and tell him, in a different way each day, how much he meant to me. Over breakfast, I'd ask him how he slept and what he had on for the day, and then I'd play his favorite song in the car and we'd sing along.

Not only did these small changes work wonders for our relationship, but they also made us both feel better about ourselves. It's amazing what a little shift can do to a person. So, here are some small things you can do in the morning that could have a big impact on your son:

- Instead of rushing around like a headless chicken in the morning, try to involve your son in some parts of the routine: make breakfast together, get ready next to each other, or eat breakfast side-by-side.
- Check in with your son in the morning, asking him how he's feeling and if he has any worries for the day ahead.
- Make mornings a technology-free time where you sit down and chat with one another or just enjoy each other's company, totally free from distractions.
- Give your son a hug, a kiss on the cheek, or tell him how much you love being his parent.
- Create a morning ritual that is unique to just you and him, or your close family unit. Perhaps you could read a story together, practice mindfulness, or do a gratitude exercise.

These are just ideas. Feel free to get creative with them.

Helping Your Son Through Peer Relationships

There is a lot of drama in kids' relationships. They fall out, they say nasty things, and at times, they can be pretty brutal. For a kid with ADHD, trying to understand and stay on top of all the nuances of social relationships can feel like trying to complete a Rubik's Cube blindfolded—tough, to say the least.

As much as we try to understand and support our kids with ADHD, not everyone gets it, and other kids aren't invested in our own sons like we are. Due to the nature of ADHD and how it can make our sons behave differently in class, it's common for kids with ADHD to be alienated or bullied for their behavior. One dad of an ADHD son said,

> "Every day there is a naughty note from school of him not listening, making and not cleaning up messes. Other kids alienating him. My mom watches him for me until I am able to get off work and she yells at him constantly for the same things. His teacher sent me an email last week stating that he broke down in tears at school because none of the other kids want to play or be near him. Tonight was the worst night. Putting him to bed he tells me that he thinks he is a bad kid because he can never do anything right, no one wants to be his friend, and all anyone does is yell at him."

As a parent, it's so hard to watch your son struggling with peer relationships and feeling alienated or being bullied at school. It's even harder when you see the impact peer relationship problems have on your son's self-confidence and mental health. Research shows that peer relationships in childhood and adolescence are vital for healthy social and emotional development. Therefore, when problems occur, this can have a big impact on our sons' mental well-being and the development of social skills (Shin et al., 2016).

Luckily, you don't have to sit by and watch this all unfold: you can make a difference to your son's peer relationships. Let's look at some of the main ways you can support your son with his friendships:

1. **Create opportunities to build friendships**

So much of making friends is opportunity. Perhaps you are in the right place at the right time, or you're pursuing an interest and you meet a like-minded person. For our sons with ADHD who struggle to form relationships, we need to create these opportunities.

Play dates are the ideal solution for preschool and elementary school-aged kiddos, as you can model what healthy social interactions look like for your son. They also give him the opportunity to play under your supervision, so you can help him learn new skills if need be. Setting up playdates with another child with ADHD is like the gold standard of all play dates, as these children will likely understand each other and get along on a deeper level, as they'll likely have similar school experiences. And meeting a parent on a similar journey to you can feel the same—they'll understand the challenges!

For older kids, encourage them to pursue their interests in a club or team. This could be anything: sports, music, board games, whatever! Find groups in your community and sign your son up to ones he likes the sound of.

2. **Work with the school**

Kids with ADHD often get a bad rep in school, but this doesn't need to be the case. If teachers can nip negative talk and any bullying in the bud and create an environment where children are kind and accepting of one another, this can drastically alter your son's experience in school.

The key is to help your son's teacher understand his ADHD diagnosis and alter their perspective to see ADHD as a difference, not a disorder, just like we did in Chapter 1. And I recommend starting as soon as you can—research shows that kids with ADHD often get a negative peer status by early-to-middle elementary school, and this can stick throughout their entire time at school.

So, work with your son's teacher and any other support staff around your son to ensure your son has the most positive school experience he can have.

Sibling Stresses: How to Help Siblings Understand

Sibling relationships are complicated, and when one sibling has an additional need like ADHD, it can bring all sorts of unique challenges. Research suggests that children with ADHD tend to have more conflict with their siblings. Plus, if ADHD is mixed with externalizing behaviors, this can often lead to less warmth and closeness between siblings (Mikami & Pfiffner, 2008).

What's more, if you have one child without ADHD and a son with ADHD, the former may struggle to understand why you treat each of them in different ways. When experts conducted interviews of this family dynamic, they found four key themes: views on differential parental treatment, discrepancy with discipline, rejection, and what is called the "parentified child", meaning the child takes the parent role.

A concept I hold dear and remind myself (and other parents) of frequently is that ADHD is a family matter. It impacts everyone in the family. Siblings will have loads of different feelings around having a brother with ADHD; some good, some bad. They may feel frustrated at the differential treatment, confused that their brother seemingly gets more attention than them, and hurt that they feel less important. As parents, it's our duty to understand the variety of emotions they may feel about the family dynamic and offer support and guidance, so they can be the most supportive brother and sister while also feeling loved and important.

Here's what you can do to make that happen:

1. Step into their shoes

Our sons with ADHD can take up a lot of space, both in our minds and in our homes. This may not leave as much space for their sibling without ADHD. So, as parents, it's important to consider the ways life may be hard for our non-ADHD child. ADHD symptoms like hyperactivity and impulsivity can disrupt the family routine, and siblings may feel frustrated by the continual disruption to their lives and the unpredictability of their brother's behavior.

What's more, if your son goes through a period of aggressive or explosive behaviors, this can be frightening for their sibling. They may be anxious, stressed, or scared that these behaviors will happen again and what they might lead to. Remember, they have no control in these situations, and that can be a scary position to be in.

They may also struggle to understand their brother's ADHD symptoms and behaviors, attributing it more to their brother's personality. This can lead to confusion, fear, or even frustration at you seemingly doing nothing about these behaviors.

Finally, a sibling of a brother with ADHD often takes on extra responsibilities as they see you struggling and often want to help. Plus, they pick up on their brother's vulnerability, and often step up to support him. While this can be super helpful, it means they have to grow up quickly. This can feel like a lot of pressure for a young child and may lead to feelings of overwhelm.

You can acknowledge that you understand all of these difficulties by openly talking to your child about it. For example, you could say, "I know how hard it can be to understand why your brother acts in certain ways, and it can be confusing and frustrating at times. I get it. I want you to know that I understand that you may have lots of different feelings about it, and you can share these with me, whatever they are. Let's talk about how you've been feeling lately." When they share their thoughts and feelings, remember to accept these non-judgmentally and problem-solve together.

2. Provide special 1:1 time

Due to the support our sons need, 1:1 time with our other children may get pushed aside. However, ensuring we make time for special 1:1 time can help our other children feel special, and it can reduce sibling conflict and rivalry. So, schedule 1:1 activities with each of your children so you can strengthen each bond, and allow them to choose what you do during that special time, as this will make it more meaningful and enjoyable for them.

Use the 1:1 time you've set aside to really listen to them, put your phone away, and be 100% present. Encourage them to share their worries and concerns with you, and talk through these non-judgmentally.

You can introduce the idea of special 1:1 time like this: "I know your brother often needs lots of special support, but I have missed spending time with just you and me. Shall we organize a time each week to have 1:1 time? You can choose what we do."

3. Settle their understanding of fairness

You want your children to be able to come to you when they feel like things are unfair or there are double standards between them and their brother. One way you can encourage this is by having family chats about fairness and equality, sharing how fairness doesn't always mean that everyone is treated the same.

You can use examples to demonstrate how different needs need different rules and approaches. For example, a paralympic athlete needs different rules and support to what an Olympic athlete does. Allow each child to share their feelings and frustrations about this, and work together as a family to problem-solve so that everyone feels respected and happy. Remember to reinforce that you love all of your children equally, even if that love may show up in different ways for each of them.

Here is one way you could broach the subject, "I've noticed that recently you have been getting upset/angry/frustrated about your brother getting to do something that I've told you that you can't. I totally understand how confusing and unfair that may feel. I want to talk about why sometimes your brother has different rules to you and why. While it may feel like it sometimes, it's not because I have a favorite. Instead, it's because each of you have different needs, and sometimes you each need me more than the other. Right now, your brother needs a lot of support, and that's why he is being treated slightly differently."

The bottom line is that ADHD is a whole family affair, and having a brother with ADHD can be hard. Understanding and acknowledging this, and ensuring you put forth effort to make your other children feel as loved and important, is vital for a happy home and strong sibling relationships.

Chapter Takeaways

- **Children with ADHD may struggle with strained relationships.** Understanding the impact ADHD may have on your bond with your son and his relationships with his peers and siblings is vital to supporting him to strengthen these bonds.
- **Building your relationship with your son doesn't have to be complicated.** It can simply involve making small changes that have a big impact, as well as taking time out to just play with your son or showing an interest in his interests.

- **For our sons with ADHD, friendships can be hard.** The constant barrage of alienation and peer rejection would take a toll on anyone, but you can support your son to develop healthy peer relationships by creating opportunities to build bonds, liaising with the school to change his teacher's perspective, and enrolling him in clubs that align with his interests.
- **ADHD is a family matter.** It doesn't just affect you and your son—it impacts everyone within the family home. Acknowledging this helps you to step into other people's shoes and support them, too.
- **Address sibling stresses head on.** Siblings who have a brother with ADHD often feel like they're left on the sidelines. By encouraging open communication, ensuring you pencil in 1:1 special time with each of your children, and educating your children on fairness and equality can help reduce sibling conflict and rivalry.

Chapter 8: Showing Your Son His Superpowers & Developing His Interests

"Sometimes the most brilliant minds do not shine in standardized tests because they do not have standardized minds."
– Diane Ravitch

Let's face it: our boys with ADHD have *a lot* of energy. It's easy for this to feel like a hindrance in everyday life, especially because life moves at 100 km an hour nowadays.

Take when my son was a toddler. Max just could not sit still, whatever anyone in kindergarten did. I was always being told that rather than sit in circle time, he was off doing something else. He was clearing up, playing with sand, or sometimes just staring out of the window. On the odd occasion that they coerced him into sitting down for circle time, he'd become overwhelmed and lash out at his classmates, kicking his legs out and hitting anyone within arm's length. So, in the end, they stopped trying to get him to join circle time at all.

I was struggling with his extreme levels of energy at home, too. Whenever we were out of the house, I was constantly telling him, "Put that down!" and "Stop, wait for me." Rarely would it seem like he was listening—he'd continue to skip ahead, distracted by seemingly anything and everything, and picking up everything in his line of sight. It was exhausting. Often, it was infuriating. So often, I would think, Why doesn't this boy listen to me?!

When we got his ADHD diagnosis, I started to feel more compassion for these behaviors, but don't get me wrong, that was still mixed in with frustration and annoyance. I just didn't know how to handle that level of impulsivity and what seemed like complete and utter defiance.

However, this fueled an interest in understanding my son's hyperactivity and impulsivity that ultimately led to us developing strategies to help him redirect his energy into positive outlets. I'll share these strategies, and ways to help your son manage his emotions, in this chapter.

Your Son's Superpowers: Seeing His ADHD Differently

Within our current society, ADHD is treated a lot like a disability, as though with an ADHD diagnosis, boys won't be able to fully develop or reach their full potential (Hai & Climie, 2022). This is far from true. Yes, the road may be bumpier, and we may have to face more hurdles, but our sons are perfectly capable of living a healthy, fulfilled life.

In fact, research indicates that our sons may even have superpowers. No, I don't mean the real, Marvel-type superpowers, but instead special abilities that can give them an edge over non-ADHDers. It's important to recognize these as parents, as we can become so bogged down in the difficulties of ADHD that we can forget to truly celebrate our children's strengths.

Here are just SOME of the strengths your son may possess *because* of his ADHD:

- **Hyperfocus**
- **Creativity**
- **High energy levels**
- **Willingness to help others**
- **Resilience**

- **Cognitive dynamism** (meaning they think differently and can shift the direction of their thinking when new information shows them that they need to change their thinking.)
- **Transcendence** (meaning their experiences go beyond the norm)
- **Problem-solving**
- **Imagination**
- **Compassion**
- *Amazing* **sense of humor!**
- **Perseverance**
- **Good at multi-tasking**
- **Accepting others & their individualities**
- **Strong sense of right and wrong**
- **High tolerance of risks**
- **Independence/self-reliance**
- **Self-awareness** (which may be gained after therapeutic interventions)
- **Impulsivity** (because it's not always a bad thing, right?!)

(ADDitude Editors, 2022; Burch, 2023; Miller et al., 2024)

Swimming legend and Olympic champion Michael Phelps is just one of many examples of people who have used their ADHD superpowers to their advantage. Phelps described to Child Mind Institute (2017) how he was always bouncing off the walls as a kid, never able to sit still. Part of the reason why Phelps loved to swim was because it stopped him from fidgeting and gave him an outlet for his energy.

Michael Phelps was told in school that he would never amount to anything or be successful. So, if he's anything to go by, our sons have just as much of a chance as anyone else with the right support!

However, let me tell you this: it's not enough to just recognize your son's strengths—you also need to use this information to develop a positive mindset towards your son's ADHD. Why? Well, because being surrounded by people with positive mindsets towards ADHD can boost children's self-esteem, and also make them feel more optimistic, less anxious and depressed, and more independent.

There are also some less obvious, but still very important, benefits of having a more positive mindset about your child's diagnosis. Research shows that a positive mindset can positively affect parents' wellbeing, as well as how satisfied they feel in their marriage (Lickenbrock, Ekas & Whitman, 2011). Trust me, it pays to be positive!

So, Phelps found his outlet: swimming. What about your son? How can you redirect his mass of energy into something positive?

Redirecting Your Son's Energy Toward Positive Outlets

Redirecting your son's energy toward positive outlets is all about adapting to make difficult tasks easier. Take homework; it can be incredibly stressful for any kid with ADHD. Having to sit still and focus for long periods of time, persevering at something that they don't immediately understand—that's tough.

One way to redirect their energy is to let them fidget. As you'll be well aware, fidgeting is common in ADHD, and it's often seen as a negative thing. However, allowing your child to fidget can make difficult tasks, where they have to sit and focus for prolonged periods, far more bearable.

Offer your son a fidget toy like a stress ball at the dinner table, when you're waiting in a queue, or while he's trying to do homework. You may notice a change in his concentration almost instantly.

Also, utilize the power of play. Play is not only important for children's development, but it also helps ADHD kids to release a lot of their pent-up energy, helping their bodies to feel tired and more settled for big tasks like chores, homework, or school. So, when you know your son has to complete a big task, schedule some play time beforehand. Play, running around, and dance are some of the best forms of play to help them regulate before a big task.

Finally, break up big tasks. I don't know about you, but even I get fidgety during a long meeting or when I'm asked to pay attention for long periods of time. Our brains need breaks, and this is even more so with our ADHD kids. Pay attention to your son's body language when he's concentrating—how long can he focus before he begins to get too distracted? It may be ten minutes, fifteen minutes, or maybe longer. Once you've noticed the pattern, you can schedule breaks in. Support him for fifteen minutes, then give him a short five-minute break to play or do some quick exercises like jumping jacks. Then, help him return to the task for another fifteen minutes before the next break.

Strategies for You to Stay Energized and Effective

You can teach your son every strategy under the sun to redirect his energy, but what about you? Let's face it: parenting a boy with ADHD is exhausting.

We spend a lot of our time in the parenting pit—the psychological place where we wonder whether we're doing the right thing, whether we're just making things worse, or if we're teaching them the right life lessons. This is often just about parenting in general, but parenting a child with ADHD brings another layer of difficulty, as extra anxiety, guilt, and fear may be mixed in with all these difficult feelings. We think: I should have done that differently, Did I deal with that in the right way?, Why do I find this so hard? You know the drill.

What's more, as parents of ADHD kids, we have to constantly be on high alert, particularly if our sons are emotionally reactive. We have to be on top of things all of the time, detecting signs that they may be dysregulated or that something is going wrong.

Let's face it, they depend on us to meet their needs more than anyone else. So, we're constantly giving them everything we've got in order to meet their needs. It's no wonder, really, that the research shows that parents of kids with ADHD are more prone to burnout and exhaustion, is it? Burnout is the state of total and utter exhaustion—physically, emotionally, and psychologically. You may be struggling with burnout if you constantly feel tired, always feel stressed, feel inadequate, isolated, or unmotivated, or you notice changes in your emotions, as well as your eating and sleeping habits.

As this role is so all-consuming and our risk of being burned out is particularly high, it's vital that we regularly implement strategies to help us stay energized so we can be the best parents for our kids and look after ourselves in the process. Let's talk about two main ways to do this:

1. Form healthy habits

Are you the type of person who wakes up early just to have some time to yourself? Who takes regular ten-minute breaks during the day to rest and recharge? No? I wasn't, either.

We've talked about how to help our sons form healthy habits, but little old you and I have been forgotten about again. Typical, right?

Remembering to form healthy habits as a parent of an ADHD kid is easier said than done—because we're not focusing on ourselves, it's easy for our healthy habits to be the first thing to slip away when times get tough or stressful.

Forming healthy habits can help you in more ways than one. Forming healthy habits helps you meet your basic human needs. For example, the three top ones are:

1. Eating well
2. Regular exercise
3. Getting quality sleep

So, eating a balanced diet is one healthy habit, and this helps boost your energy throughout the day so you can parent in the way you want to. Going out for a morning walk is another habit, and this one will help you meet your exercise needs, which can have many benefits for your cardiovascular system, immune system, metabolism, and circulation, as well as curbing symptoms of anxiety and depression. Taking care of your sleep by, say, keeping a consistent bedtime and ensuring that when you go to sleep, you get good-quality sleep (by reducing exposure to blue light before bed, getting black-out blinds, and so on); this can help you feel well-rested and more resilient in the day ahead (Gordon & Barnes, 2020).

Habits can also help you set a good example for your son, especially if you're trying to instill healthy habits in him. Just as I talked about with modeling, your healthy habits play a big role in influencing your son's behavior, as our kids learn what to eat, how often to exercise, and so on from us.

Can you see the difference here? By incorporating a couple of small, healthy habits into your day, you can completely change how restful your day feels.

2. Prioritize self-care once in a while

There's a whole chapter on self-care yet to come, so I won't go into the nitty gritty of it here. But I will say this: self-care may feel selfish, but it's a vital part of maintaining our energy, well-being, and also our ability to look after others.

Taking care of ourselves allows us to take care of others. Think about it—when you add up all of the energy needed when looking after any child, let alone a child with additional needs, your battery is drained. There's nothing left in the tank.

Caring for a son with ADHD can be like a full-time job, with the therapies, additional support, tantrums, teaching him extra skills at home, and all manner of other things! So, we need to treat it as such. And what do you do when you have a full-time job? You take a holiday. That doesn't mean to say dropping your responsibilities and jet setting off for Mexico. I simply mean that you deserve some consistent self-care. But more on this in Chapter 10.

Chapter Takeaways

- **Your son has strengths. Recognize and celebrate these.** Yes, many challenges come with an ADHD diagnosis, but your son also possesses many strengths and abilities that he may not have otherwise had. From hyperfocus to compassion to intense creativity, your son's superpowers should be celebrated as this will empower him and enhance his potential.
- **Identify your negative mindset.** Shifting your perspective from viewing ADHD as a disability to a difference with strengths and drawbacks will help you feel less bogged down by the diagnosis and give your son better self-esteem.
- **Your son has so much energy, so use it.** Your son is a big ol' ball of energy, so instead of letting this go to waste, use it to help him. Let him fidget, utilize the power of play, and give him plenty of breaks.
- **Stay energized by forming healthy habits and practicing self-care.** You can't look after others if you're not looking after yourself. Form healthy habits and use self-care to keep yourself energized and excited to parent your son.

Chapter 9: Planning for Changes & Transitions

"When I approach a child, he inspires in me two sentiments — tenderness for what he is and respect for what he may become."
– Louis Pasteur

None of us really like change, do we? Change is a difficult but inevitable part of life, as constant as the tide moving in and out. When you're the parent of a son with ADHD, changes and transitions are a whole other ball game. What I mean is: they suck. They can feel like navigating the worst of weather blindfolded.

And life is full of transitions, particularly for kids. Some of them are expected, like moving from elementary school to middle school, and middle to high school. On the other hand, some can be sudden—such as your son's favorite teacher leaving abruptly, or his weekly routine being disrupted by bad weather. For ADHD sons, any and all changes and transitions can be tough, as they shake the foundation of their routine, a part of their life that makes them feel safe and in control.

As much as we'd love to shield our sons from the difficulties that changes and transitions bring, we can't stop them from happening. However, what we can do is prepare them as best we can for when these changes happen: giving them coping strategies for managing.

So, in this chapter, I'll delve into the unique difficulties that boys with ADHD can encounter when it comes to dealing with change and transitions head on. We already recognize that transitions are hard, but *why* they're hard, and how this relates to boys' ADHD, I'll cover in more depth throughout this chapter.

Along the way, I'll sprinkle in some scripts and practical strategies to help you support your son in pivotal moments, whether it's preparing for a transition into a new environment or guiding him through the challenges of adolescence and the transition into adulthood. By the end of this chapter, you'll have the tools you need to help your son every step of the way.

Transitions are daunting; that's a fact. However, with the right prep and support, they can be turned into an opportunity for learning and growth, rather than something to dread. So, shall we?

Transitioning to New Environments

Transitioning to new environments is no walk in the park when you're a kid with ADHD. And the reason for this? Well, it's those same old executive functions that are the main reason. A vital part of successfully adapting to transitions is being able to plan, organize, and think flexibly, altering our plans and way of approaching a situation as it changes.

Fortunately for some of us, our abilities to plan and organize ourselves in the face of changes and transitions make us feel more in control. We can change tack, thinking: Ah, I can't do that anymore, but maybe I could do this? However, our sons with ADHD struggle more with these skills because of their difficulties with executive functions in general.

A big part of transitions is also regulating our difficult feelings that crop up around change. Let's be honest, none of us enjoys change. We are creatures of habit; we get comfortable with what we're used to, and the familiar feels safer.

So, when something comes in and alters this familiarity, we end up feeling a bit dysregulated.

These aren't the only two reasons why our sons find transitions particularly tricky. They also have those sensory triggers we spoke about way back in Chapter 3. Our sons' sensory triggers can make new environments particularly overwhelming and anxiety-inducing, and the unpredictability of these environments, as well as having no clue what an unknown environment is going to be like, can send our kids into meltdown pretty sharpish.

There is a way to get around the whole new environment situation. And no, it's not "Never leaving the house" so don't worry! Instead, it combines a technique from a therapy approach called exposure therapy, and building structure.

Strategy 1: Exposure Therapy: Exposure & Desensitization

If we think about it, new environments can be incredibly daunting. There are so many new things to see, hear, smell, and touch, that it's not a wonder our sons with ADHD find them challenging.

Gradual exposure and desensitization, a technique from exposure therapy, helps our sons slowly get used to new environments, building up their confidence at their own pace. It's very similar to when you go swimming outdoors: you dip your toe in the water first to check it's not going to give you hypothermia, then slowly you put your leg, then your stomach, and finally your shoulders under the water.

So, to expose your son to a new environment slowly, start by showing him pictures of what the place looks like. Your own photos would be great if you can go there ahead of time, as this will make it seem more familiar. Then talk through the types of sounds and smells your son might experience there.

Then take him to the place when it's closed or practically empty. This will give him time to get used to the general feel of it before he has to go there when it's busier. Finally, when he feels comfortable enough to go, bring some coping strategies for him, such as a squishy ball, noise defenders, sunglasses, etc.

Strategy 2: Building Structure: Make It Predictable

You may not be able to make the new environment predictable (although exposure and desensitization really help!), but you can make the structure *around* the visit predictable. For example, ensure you have a consistent daily routine in place, and schedule the visit to the new environment ahead of time so your son can get used to the idea (for example, on a visual timetable).

If you have the time, create a little routine around the visit. Perhaps, start by going to his favorite shop or to eat his favorite breakfast, drive by the new place, and then do a preferred activity afterwards, like going trampolining. Then, the next time, keep this routine the same, but this time go into the new place.

Building familiarity and structure around visiting a new place will reduce your son's anxiety, and doing something he loves before and after the visit helps sweeten the sting of having to experience something new.

One other factor that makes it difficult for our sons to manage transitions and change is that they struggle to inhibit their impulses. This means that they can be more distracted and struggle to focus, which can make it particularly hard when they have to switch from one task to another. This is possibly the most evident when it involves moving from a task our sons love, to one they don't love quite so much—I'm talking about a video-games-to-clearing- up kind of transition. Yep, you know the score.

TRANSITIONING FROM PREFERRED TO NON-PREFERRED TASKS

Picture this: Max is age twelve. He's at home on a Saturday morning playing video games. He's been online with his friends for a couple of hours now. I tell him, "Hey Max, you've got ten more minutes on the video games, then it's time to tidy your room." Now, for the record—this isn't something I've just sprung on him—this little dance is something we do every Saturday morning. Unfortunately, it kept on getting into the same pattern.

I'm met with moaning and grumbling. Then he tries to get out of it, saying he only did it last week, and it's really not that messy. I look around … yes, it really is that messy. But he continues to grumble. I empathize with him but remind him that he still needs to keep his room tidy. Then, the ten minutes are up, and I let him know. Whoosh! It's that fast, and he's angry. He's yelling at me to leave him alone, and tries to slam the door in my face.

Ever experienced something similar? There's something about getting our ADHD sons to switch from doing an activity they love to doing a task they can't stand that gets them super worked up. A few years ago, I found out why.

According to a clinical psychologist, kids with ADHD have less active reward centers in their brains. In other words, they find tasks less rewarding than we do throughout the day. However, when something *is* rewarding (like video games, in this instance), they hyper-focus on it, which means they can sit and do it for hours. Then, when we ask them to do something that they find less rewarding, we're met with resistance. As our kids often struggle to regulate their emotions in moments like this, it can end in an emotional blow up.

I tried so many things when getting my son to transition from a preferred to a non-preferred task, but there was only one thing that worked. *One*! It was: giving each task a soundtrack.

Songs can be really helpful for kids with ADHD to build associations. For example, say you always put a particular song on when it's time to tidy their room. Well, over time, their brains will build an association with that particular song and the action. So, when you play the song, they'll perform the action.

There are so many songs out there for preschool and kindergarten kids, but it is not so easy finding one for older kids. If I had played Max's clean-up song from kindergarten when he was twelve, I'd have likely been met with even more rage. So, instead, you can invite them to create a playlist or soundtrack for each task. Perhaps it's a song they love or something that makes them want to get up and get moving. For older kids, ensure they have a little bit of control over the song, and also, you can task them with putting it on if you think they will. As we know, older kids want as much independence as they can get.

Giving them more independence is just one of the ways we can help our kids transition into adolescence and adulthood. More on this next.

Preparing for Adolescence

Adolescence is a time that many of we as parents dread. I'm talking about all of us, not just you and I, with a son with ADHD. It's a time of massive physical, emotional, and psychological changes, and navigating these ups and downs can be incredibly hard, both as a parent and for the teen involved.

For kids with ADHD, adolescence can be a particularly tumultuous time. Our sons with ADHD may already struggle with mood swings and difficulties regulating their emotions, so the hormone changes in adolescence may only serve to heighten these. Of course, this can have a massive impact, not just on our sons but on the family as a whole.

Then you throw socializing into the mix. Social relationships become ever-more important when kids reach adolescence. In fact, they become more important to our kids than our relationship with them (Telzer et al., 2015). In this time, peer relationships are their primary form of social support (Furman & Buhrmester, 1992).

As adolescence is a time of such drastic changes, it pays to be prepared. So, here are my three top tips for preparing your son for adolescence:

1. Set Permeable Boundaries

Adolescence is a time when our sons are trying to figure out so much: who they are, how they fit into the world, who is important to them, what kind of adult they want to be, and so much more. The last thing they want is to not know where they stand with us.

So, we have to be consistent, and one way to do this is through setting boundaries. Now, these boundaries have to be firm and clear. However, they need to be permeable, too. What I mean by this is that there needs to be a to and fro between you and your son. He's old enough now to know (partly) what he wants, but you're still the adult who needs to guide. So, agree on boundaries together as much as possible. Then, when you implement them, they won't come as a surprise.

When setting boundaries, remember to clearly communicate your expectations and validate your son's feelings when he finds it difficult to adhere to them.

2. Expand Their Understanding Over Time

If we don't teach our sons about important topics like puberty and adolescence, who will? My motto is: if my son isn't getting the information from me, he'll source it somewhere else. With the amount of false information out there, it's far better to control the information your son is getting. So, along that vein, it's just easier to tell him yourself.

Openly discuss puberty as well as the physical, emotional, and hormonal changes that come with adolescence with your son. Offer age-appropriate information about body changes, sexual health, and reproductive anatomy, keeping it factual.

3. **Encourage Their Independence**

Most of the time, as our sons reach adolescence, they're crying out for independence. So, what can we do? Well, we can give it to them, in healthy doses.

Now, I know how hard this is when you have a son with ADHD. You've had to protect him for so long and support him every step of the way, that it can be so hard to let go. It can come with a whole range of emotions, but especially anxiety about whether he'll be okay as an independent young man. If this is you, just take it a step at a time.

Start by allowing your son to take on more responsibilities and make decisions independently, then gradually expand his freedom as he shows more maturity. For example, as he becomes more confident, encourage him to take ownership of things like managing his schoolwork and his belongings, and planning activities he wants to do.

Once you've overcome the hurdle of adolescence, there's no rest, I'm afraid. It's straight onto transitioning into adulthood. Yippee!

Transitioning into Adulthood

Just like our young sons transitioning into adolescence can pose challenges, so too can their journey into adulthood. However, the obstacles in their path take on a slightly different form. As our sons prepare to enter adulthood, they rely on us for guidance, support, and encouragement, looking to us to identify whether they are capable of beginning to navigate life on their own.

So, in this crucial stage of life, we need to show that we believe in them and that they are capable. However, this doesn't mean leaving them to their own devices. Our sons still need support, but what kind?

Here is the main form of support our sons need from us as they transition into adulthood:

1. Teach Practical Life Skills

When our sons fly the nest, we want them to be prepared, and the way to do this is through teaching life skills. Life skills are never more important than when we begin the transition into adulthood. However, we don't have to wait until they're on the brink of adulthood to teach them. Teaching life skills can begin at any age, right from inviting them to help you cook and clean to getting them to clear up after themselves.

One book I read that changed my perception of getting kids to help out around the house was *Hunt, Gather, Parent* by Michaeleen Doucleff, PhD (2021). In her book, Doucleff explores the differences between individualist communities like those in the Western world and collectivist communities such as Inuit families above the Arctic Circle. She shares much guidance on how to get your kids to help out around the house, but I'll discuss what stuck with me the most.

Teaching your kids life skills doesn't have to be a chore. If you get it right, they'll volunteer to help. However, you've got to tap into their natural initiative to help. You can do this in two ways:

1. **Let them help whenever they show an interest.** Start by allowing them to help out in whatever they show an interest in, even if it'll take longer to finish the task or they'll likely make a mess of it. Letting them help is a sign that you believe they're competent and capable.
2. **Frame chores as a family affair.** Rather than telling your son, "Go wash your dishes" (which no son with ADHD wants to hear, by the way), frame the task as a communal activity. For example, "Let's work together to get the dishes done." Then, while you're doing the task, "We get through the dishes so fast when we do them together." See the difference?

Small changes like this can tap into our children's natural inclination to help and encourage them to build life skills without us badgering or lecturing them. Check out Doucleff's book; I highly recommend it!

Chapter Takeaways

- **Change is inevitable, but transitions can be hard.** Although changes and transitions are an unavoidable part of life, it doesn't make them any easier, particularly for boys with ADHD. Understanding why transitions can be tough for our sons is the first step to supporting them when they face these changes.
- **Executive functions are essential for transitions & changes.** We need our executive functions such as planning, organization, and emotional regulation to manage changes and transitions, so it's not a wonder our sons struggle with these.
- **Try at-home exposure therapy and building structure.** Gradual exposure and desensitization, as well as building structure around transitions, can help our sons navigate these tricky situations.
- **Managing transitions from preferred to non-preferred tasks often sucks.** Yet, they can be a little less sucky when we utilize the power of music. Allocating a song to each task helps our sons create an association, so when the music plays, their brains naturally want to get up and get the task done.
- **Adolescence is a big transition.** Yet, we can help our sons tackle these transitions by setting permeable boundaries, expanding their understanding of puberty and adolescence, and encouraging their independence.
- **Transitioning into adulthood requires life skills.** Teaching your son practical life skills will be vital in his transition into adulthood. So, tap into his natural inclination to help and make household chores a family affair.

Chapter 10:
Mastering the Art of Self-Care When You Have a Son with ADHD

"Self-care is giving the world the best of you, instead of what's left of you."
– Katie Reed

As parents of a son with ADHD, we're no strangers to sacrifice. There are so many hours spent at appointments, speaking with our son's teachers, liaising with therapists, and perhaps the biggest one of all, worrying about our son and just taking care of him. In the middle of all this, our own needs tend to take the backseat. If you think of a long, long to-do list written on a scroll, our wants and needs would be rolled out 1,000 yards down the road.

For us, time is a commodity, and energy is fleeting. So, when I mention "self-care", you'll rightly think, Yeah, what a luxury.

Yet, self-care shouldn't be a luxury. It shouldn't be relegated to the very end of the to-do list. Self-care is a fundamental aspect of effective parenting. By investing in ourselves and our own well-being, we replenish our reserves of resilience, strength, patience, and calmness, making way for the difficult emotions that come up as a parent of a son with ADHD. But it's more than this—it also models healthy habits for our sons.

So, in this tenth and final chapter, I'll storm through self-care and how to master the art of taking care of yourself. First, I'll dig a little deeper into how caring for yourself makes you a better parent, because I reckon you need a little more convincing.

How Caring for Yourself Makes You a Better Parent

When you're parenting a child with ADHD who depends on you all of the time, self-care may feel selfish. However, let me put it this way: when we care for other people 24/7 and never take a break or time for ourselves, it's like trying to pour water from an empty cup (Godman, 2023). It's impossible—and so is trying to meet your son's needs at all times without taking time out.

For a second, imagine your well-being as that cup. Throughout the day, as you get your son up and ready for school, send him off on his way, do whatever you do in the day, whether it's working, the household chores, taking care of younger children, and so on. For every task, you pour a little bit out of your cup. Some tasks demand a lot of the liquid in your cup, while others only take a little bit. Slowly, slowly, slowly, throughout the day, your cup gets emptier and emptier.

Without replenishing it, what are you going to do? You can't keep on giving resources when you don't have. You may find yourself running on fumes, your reserves feeling completely depleted, and your ability to manage difficult situations thrown out the window.

Then self-care comes along and fills that cup back up, ensuring you have all the emotional reserves you need to handle the day-to-day of parenting. When you think of it this way, self-care isn't a luxury—it's a necessity. By taking care of your well-being, you can continue to offer all of the love and support you give to others. When you don't top up your reserves, you run the risk of burnout, depression, anxiety, and physical illnesses.

Just think about why, on airplanes, they tell you to put on your oxygen mask before trying to help anyone else. Without air yourself, you can't help anyone. By meeting your own needs once in a while, you can help your son and meet his needs with the empathy, understanding, and patience you aspire to.

THE ART OF SELF-CARE

One of the common misconceptions that parents have when I talk about self-care is that they imagine a luxurious spa weekend or an evening away. While this does classify as self-care and sounds wonderful, this may not feel in any way attainable.

Self-care doesn't have to be anything extravagant. It can simply be five or ten minutes at the beginning of the day to drink your coffee or time to yourself after your son has gone to sleep.

Here are some self-care ideas for busy parents of ADHD kids:

10-minute morning meditation	15-minute stretches or yoga	Journaling for 5 minutes in the morning	Daily morning walk (outside or on a treadmill indoors)	Spending 10 minutes alone in the garden
Cooking yourself a nutritious meal	Texting or calling a friend	Reading 10 pages of a leisure book	Listening to your favorite song	Mindful eating
Setting boundaries with your son (more on this later)	1-hour therapy session a week	Starting the day with positive affirmations	Taking a break from social media	4-minute deep breathing exercises

Listening to a mindfulness meditation before bed	Going for a walk in nature	Doing your hobby for 15 minutes a day	Taking a long bath	Going for a fortnightly massage
Keeping a gratitude jar/journal	Burning incense or essential oils	Spending 10 minutes doing nothing	Getting a good night's sleep	Commit to a morning or nighttime routine
Get dressed	Listen to an inspirational podcast	Say "no" to something you don't want to do	Declutter an area of your home that's causing you stress	Try progressive muscle relaxation

Remember, self-care isn't about indulging in occasional luxuries. It's about integrating these small self-care practices consistently into your daily or weekly routine. These acts replenish our emotional reserves and equip us with the strength and resilience we need to navigate the challenges of parenting a son with ADHD.

I want to leave you with one final message. As you start your self-care journey, know that self-care isn't about perfection; you likely won't implement self-care straight away and be perfect at it for the rest of time. Sometimes, we start to add self-care practices in, but when the going gets tough, they fall off the face of the Earth.

It's okay. You don't need to be hard on yourself about this as well as everything else. Self-care is about progress, not perfection. So, start small, be kind to yourself, and celebrate each moment you dedicate to nurturing yourself. You never know; you might surprise yourself with the kind of parent you become.

Chapter Takeaways

- **Self-care isn't a luxury; it's essential.** As parents of a son with ADHD, it's easy to focus on our sons wholeheartedly and forget to take care of ourselves. Yet self-care is vital in replenishing our emotional reserves and helping us stay resilient to the everyday difficulties of parenting a boy with ADHD.
- **Ensure you fill up your emotional cup.** You're so good at filling the cup of everyone else around you; make sure you take time to fill up your emotional cup, too. When your cup is empty, it's tricky to be the type of parent you want to be.
- **Self-care strategies don't have to be extravagant.** They can be something tiny and seemingly insignificant, like taking five minutes to look out of the window while you drink your morning coffee.
- **It's all about progress, not perfection.** Self-care is a journey, not a destination. So, it's normal for us to stumble and forget about self-care when life gets difficult. Remember to take small steps and be kind to yourself every step of the way.

* * *

To help you stick to your self-care routine, scan the QR code below to unlock your final bonus toolkit, the **Self-Care Planner for Parents.**

This is a detailed planner for parents of boys with ADHD, including calendars, self-care routines, goal trackers, and mindfulness exercises to support your own well-being and maintain a balanced life while managing your child's needs.

Wrapping It Up

We know better than most that parenting a son with ADHD takes patience, dedication, and support every step along the way. Throughout this guide, we've traveled through the journey of parenting a son with ADHD, right from understanding the ins and outs of an ADHD diagnosis to building strategies to help our sons navigate life.

We've changed our perspective on what ADHD is and what our sons are capable of, focusing on ADHD as a difference, not a disorder, and helping find ways to communicate this with others. And we've delved into the minefield of diagnosis and treatment options to understand how best to get our sons over this tricky hurdle.

In each chapter, we've explored a different challenge that each of us knows all too well. You've learned how to help your son manage his sensory triggers, build healthy, supportive relationships, control his intense emotions, boost his executive function and problem-solving skills, and tackle changes and transitions.

Finally, you've learned what it means to take care of yourself, not by taking a luxury spa weekend away (although please do that, if you can—you deserve it), but by making the most of small moments and filling your cup in the ways you need the most.

Now, for my final word for you and all parents supporting sons with ADHD, from one parent to another. Parenting a son with ADHD is one of the biggest challenges we will likely ever face. We often find ourselves bogged down in the negatives, finding it difficult to see the wood from the trees, but with the 100s of 1000s of challenges we face, there is growth, learning, and love.

So, as you finish this book, I invite you to reflect on how far you and your son have come. Think of the countless hours you've spent supporting your son, advocating for him. Those sleepless nights filled with worry, the meltdowns, the breakdowns, the anxiety, but also the moments of connection. The times of pure joy that keep you going. Seeing your son smile, and feeling that sense of victory when you get it right.

While so much may have changed for you and your son, two things have stayed the same: your dedication and unwavering love for him. Know that your efforts don't go unnoticed, although it may feel like it. Your son sees and feels your love and dedication. He hears your words of encouragement, even if he rolls his eyes or shrugs it off. Don't underestimate the power of your constant support, for it is powerful beyond belief.

As you continue on your journey, remember the power of your love and dedication. While there are undoubtedly challenges ahead of you, you have tackled many difficulties before, and you *can* manage anything else that's thrown your way. Your son will be okay; you'll make sure of it.

THANK YOU

Thank you so much for choosing my book.

Among the many options available, your decision to pick this one is truly appreciated.

So THANK YOU for selecting this book and for reaching the very end!

Before you close the book, I have a small favor to ask, please. Would you kindly consider leaving a review? Your feedback is invaluable and helps me continue writing content that resonates with you. I'm deeply grateful for your support and look forward to hearing from you.

I truly hope that this book serves as a valuable resource for your parenting journey, and that you enjoyed reading it as much as I enjoyed writing it.

Please scan the QR code below to leave a review on Amazon:

References

American Psychological Association (2022). *Diagnostic and Statistical Manual of Mental Disorders: DSM-5-TR*. American Psychiatric Association Publishing.

Centers for Disease Control and Prevention (2022, June 8). Data and statistics about ADHD. https://www.cdc.gov/ncbddd/adhd/data.html

Kofler, M., Irwin, L. N., Soto, E. F., Groves, N. B., Harmon, S. L., & Sarver, D. E. (2018). "Executive functioning heterogeneity in pediatric ADHD." *Journal of Abnormal Child Psychology*, 47(2), 273–286. https://doi.org/10.1007/s10802-018-0438-2

Goldstein, S., & Naglieri, J. A. (Eds.). (2014). *Handbook of Executive Functioning*. Springer Science + Business Media. https://doi.org/10.1007/978-1-4614-8106-5

Kofler, M., Irwin, L. N., Soto, E. F., Groves, N. B., Harmon, S. L., & Sarver, D. E. (2018b). "Executive functioning heterogeneity in pediatric ADHD." *Journal of Abnormal Child Psychology*, 47(2), 273–286. https://doi.org/10.1007/s10802-018-0438-2

Langberg, J. M., & Epstein, J. N. (2009). "Non-pharmacological approaches for treating children with ADHD inattentive type." *F1000 Medicine Reports, 1*, 16. https://doi.org/10.3410/M1-16

Substance Abuse and Mental Health Services Administration. (2016). *DSM-5 Changes: Implications for Child Serious Emotional Disturbance.* Substance Abuse and Mental Health Services Administration (US).

Attention-Deficit/Hyperactivity Disorder (ADHD) in Children. (n.d.). Johns Hopkins Medicine. https://www.hopkinsmedicine.org/health/conditions-and-diseases/adhdadd

Mikami, A. Y. (2021). *Friendship Problems? How Parents Can Help.* CHADD. https://chadd.org/adhd-news/adhd-news-caregivers/friendship-problems-how-parents-can-help/#:~:text=Problems%20getting%20along%20with%20peers,go%20on%20year%20after%20year.

Lickenbrock, D. M., Ekas, N. V., & Whitman, T. L. (2011). "Feeling good, feeling bad: Influences of maternal perceptions of the child and marital adjustment on well-being in mothers of children with an autism spectrum disorder." *Journal of autism and developmental disorders, 41,* 848-858.

Hai, T., & Climie, E. A. (2022). "Positive child personality factors in children with ADHD." *Journal of Attention Disorders, 26*(3), 476-486.

ADDitude Editors. (2022, July 22). "What I Would Never Trade Away." ADDitude Magazine. https://www.additudemag.com/slideshows/positives-of-adhd/

Burch, K. (2023, December 11). "10 Surprising Benefits of Having ADHD." Verywellhealth. https://www.verywellhealth.com/benefits-of-adhd-strengths-and-superpowers-5210520

Miller, C., Jelinkova, K., Charabin, E., & Climie, E. A. (2024). "Parent and Child-Reported Strengths of Children with ADHD." *Canadian*

Journal of School Psychology.
https://doi.org/10.1177/08295735231225261

McGonigal, K. (2013, June). "How to make stress your friend" [Video]. TED Conferences.
https://www.ted.com/talks/kelly_mcgonigal_how_to_make_stress_your_friend

ADHD Foundation. (2022). "Emotion Regulation in Young Children."
https://www.adhdfoundation.org.uk/wp-content/uploads/2022/05/Emotion-regulation-in-young-children.pdf

Fidelity Charitable (2023, November 4). "Study shows that more than 80% of parents find success in modeling philanthropic behavior for their children—growing the next generation of givers."
https://www.fidelitycharitable.org/about-us/news/study-shows-that-more-than-80-percent-of-parents-find-success-in-modeling-philanthropic-behavior.html

Bertin, M. (2023, February 8). "Your Child's Brain on Mindful Meditation." ADDitude. https://www.additudemag.com/mindfulness-meditation-for-kids-with-adhd/

Gordon, A. M., & Barnes, C. M. (2020, March 31). "How Working Parents Can Prioritize Sleep." *Harvard Business Journal.*
https://hbr.org/2020/03/how-working-parents-can-prioritize-sleep#:~:text=Set%20a%20consistent%20sleep%20routine,fall%20asleep%20and%20stay%20asleep.

Godman, H. (2023, January 26). "Pouring from an empty cup? Three ways to refill emotionally." Harvard Health Publishing.
https://www.health.harvard.edu/blog/pouring-from-an-empty-cup-three-ways-to-refill-emotionally-202301262882

Still, G.F. (1902). "Some abnormal psychical conditions in children." *Lancet (1),* 1008–1012, 1077–1082.

"Data and statistics about ADHD"CDC. (2022b, June 8). Centers for Disease Control and Prevention. https://www.cdc.gov/ncbddd/adhd/data.html#:~:text=Millions%20of%20US%20children%20have%20been%20diagnosed%20with%20ADHD&text=Boys%20(13%25)%20are%20more,ADHD%20than%20girls%20(6%25).

"ADD Symptoms in Boys vs. Girls – What are the Differences?" Drake Institute. (n.d.). https://www.drakeinstitute.com/add-in-boys-vs-girls

Romeo, J. (2021, July 20). ADHD: "The History of a Diagnosis." JSTOR DAILY. https://daily.jstor.org/adhd-the-history-of-a-diagnosis/

Gunnerson, T. (2022, August 25). "A Brief History of ADHD." WebMD. https://www.webmd.com/add-adhd/adhd-history

"What Types of Treatment Do Children with ADHD Receive?" (2018, September 28). Centers for Disease Control and Prevention. https://www.cdc.gov/ncbddd/adhd/features/kf-national-treatment-profile-adhd-nsdata.html

Oxford Reference. (n.d.). "Deficit model." https://www.oxfordreference.com/view/10.1093/oi/authority.20110803095707115.

Johnston, C., & Chronis-Tuscano, A. (2015). "Families and ADHD." In R. A. Barkley (Ed.), *Attention-Deficit Hyperactivity Disorder: A Handbook for Diagnosis and Treatment* (4th ed., pp. 191–209). The Guilford Press.

Street, F. (2021, February 5). "Carol Dweck: A Summary of Growth and Fixed Mindsets." Farnam Street. https://fs.blog/carol-dweck-mindset/

Vitulano, L. A., Mitchell, J. T., Vitulano, M. L., Leckman, J. F., Saunders, D., Davis, N., Woodward, D., Goodhue, B., Artukoglu, B., & Kober, H. (2022). "Parental perspectives on attention-deficit/hyperactivity disorder treatments for children." *Clinical Child Psychology and Psychiatry*, 27(4), 1019–1032. https://doi.org/10.1177/13591045221108836

Zwi, M., Jones, H., Thorgaard, C., York, A., & Dennis, J. A. (2011). "Parent training interventions for Attention Deficit Hyperactivity Disorder (ADHD) in children aged 5 to 18 years." Cochrane Library. https://doi.org/10.1002/14651858.cd003018.pub3

Jensen, P. S. (1999). "A 14-month randomized clinical trial of treatment strategies for attention-deficit/hyperactivity disorder." Archives of *General Psychiatry*, 56(12), 1073-1086. https://doi.org/10.1001/archpsyc.56.12.1073

Kamal, M., Eltohami, M., Al-Shibli, S., & Khan, S. (2018). "Effect and side effect of stimulant/methylphenidate on children and adolescents with ADHD: the Qatar experience." Arch Pediatr: JPED-160. DOI, 10.

Villines, Z. (2021, June 29). "What to do if a child with ADHD cannot sleep." Medical News Today. https://www.medicalnewstoday.com/articles/adhd-child-sleep#:~:text=Most%20studies%20on%20the%20subject,cause%2C%20according%20to%20this%20research.

WebMD Editorial Contributors. (2023, February 16). "Complementary and Alternative Treatments for Childhood ADHD." WebMD. https://www.webmd.com/add-adhd/childhood-adhd/adhd-alternative-treatments

Lopes, V. (2023, October 31). "Is it common for kids with ADHD to have great behavior at school and difficult behavior at home?" Child Mind Institute. https://childmind.org/article/is-it-common-for-kids-with-adhd-to-have-great-behavior-at-school-and-difficult-behavior-at-home/#:~:text=These%20demands%20can%20be%20difficult,seeking%20behaviors%20you're%20describing.

Still, G. F. (1902). "Some abnormal psychical conditions in children." *Lancet.*

Bhandari, S. (2022, August 25). "A Brief History of ADHD." WebMD. https://www.webmd.com/add-adhd/adhd-history

Crusher, A. (2017, November 20). "What clutter does to your brain." ADD CrusherTM. ADD Crusher. https://addcrusher.com/what-clutter-does-to-your-brain/

"What we do and why." Children's University. (n.d.). https://www.childrensuniversity.co.uk/about-us/what-we-do-and-why/#:~:text=By%20the%20time%20a%20child,most%20of%20the%20remaining%2091%25.

Christenson, S. L., & Sheridan, S. M. (2001). *School and families: Creating essential connections for learning.* New York, NY: Guilford Press

Hendersen, A. T., & Mapp, K. L. (2002). *A new wave of evidence: The impact of school, family and community connections on students' achievement.* Austin, TX: Southwest Educational Laboratory.

Braley, C. (2012). "Parent-teacher partnerships in Special Education. Honors Projects Overview." Paper 65. http://digitalcommons.ric.edu/honors_projects/65.

Taylor, R. L., Smiley, L. R., & Richards, S. B. (2009). *Exceptional students: Preparing teachers for the 21st century.* New York, NY: McGraw-Hill.

Welch, M., & Sheridan, S. M. (1995). *Educational partnerships: Serving students at risk.* Fort Worth, TX: Harcourt Brace.

Johnston, C., Mash, E. J., Miller, N., & Ninowski, J. E. (2012). "Parenting in adults with attention-deficit/hyperactivity disorder (ADHD)." *Clinical Psychology Review*, 32(4), 215–228. https://doi.org/10.1016/j.cpr.2012.01.007

Queensland Health. (2022, July 15). "Sensory overload is real and can affect any combination of the body's five senses: learn ways to deal with it." https://www.health.qld.gov.au/newsroom/features/sensory-overload-is-real-and-can-affect-any-combination-of-the-bodys-five-senses-learn-ways-to-deal-with-it#:~:text=Sensory%20overload%20is%20when%20your,%2C%20flight%2C%20or%20freeze%20mode.

Green, R. (2022, August 6). "Overstimulation in ADHD." Verywellmind. https://www.verywellmind.com/adhd-symptom-spotlight-overstimulation-5323859#:~:text=Overstimulation%20is%20a%20state%20of,or%20process%20anything%20that's%20happening.

Bijlenga, D., Tjon-Ka-Jie, J. Y. M., Schuijers, F., & Kooij, J. J. S. (2017). "Atypical sensory profiles as core features of adult ADHD, irrespective of autistic symptoms." *European Psychiatry: T Journal of the Association of European Psychiatrists, 43*, 51–57. https://doi.org/10.1016/j.eurpsy.2017.02.481

Mae, A. (2023, November 13). "What to know about ADHD and sensory overload." Medical News Today. https://www.medicalnewstoday.com/articles/adhd-sensory-overload

Rausch, V. H., Bauch, E. M., & Bunzeck, N. (2014). "White noise improves learning by modulating activity in dopaminergic midbrain regions and right superior temporal sulcus." *Journal of Cognitive Neuroscience*, 26(7), 1469–1480. https://doi.org/10.1162/jocn_a_00537

Angwin, A. J., Wilson, W. J., Arnott, W. L., Signorini, A., Barry, R. J., & Copland, D. A. (2017). "White noise enhances new-word learning in healthy adults." *Scientific Reports*, 7(1). https://doi.org/10.1038/s41598-017-13383-3

"Low Gain Hearing Aids" – HearSay Speech and Hearing Centre. (n.d.). https://www.hearsay.ca/low-gain-hearing-aids/#:~:text=Low%2Dgain%20hearing%20aids%20can%20be%20an%20effective%20treatment%20for%3A&text=Hyperacusis%20(hypersensitivity%20to%20sound%20and,Sensory%20processing%20disorders%2C%20Autism%2C%20ADHD

Beck, C. (2023, June 21). "Sensory Brushing." The OT Toolbox. https://www.theottoolbox.com/sensory-brushing/

Olivardio, R. (2024, April 8). "Got a Picky Eater on Your Hands? Here's How to Cope." ADDitude. https://www.additudemag.com/picky-eaters-adhd-food-children/

Herbert, J. (2023, March 17). "ADHD and Emotional Dysregulation: Support for Navigating Life's Challenges." Beyond Booksmart. https://www.beyondbooksmart.com/executive-functioning-strategies-blog/adhd-emotional-dysregulation#:~:text=In%20ADHD%20individuals%2C%20research%20suggests,motivation%2C%20in%20the%20prefrontal%20cortex.

Dr. Dan Siegel. (2017, August 9). "Dr. Dan Siegel's Hand Model of the Brain" [Video]. YouTube. https://www.youtube.com/watch?v=f-m2YcdMdFw

Spencer T. J. (2006). "ADHD and Comorbidity in Childhood." *The Journal of Clinical Psychiatry*, 67 Suppl 8, 27–31.

Reale, L., Bartoli, B., Cartabia, M., Zanetti, M., Costantino, M. A., Canevini, M. P., Termine, C., Bonati, M., & Lombardy ADHD Group (2017). "Comorbidity prevalence and treatment outcome in children and adolescents with ADHD." European Child & Adolescent Psychiatry, 26(12), 1443–1457. https://doi.org/10.1007/s00787-017-1005-z

"ADHD and Co-Occurring Conditions." CHADD. (2019, January 4).https://chadd.org/about-adhd/co-occuring-conditions/

Leitner Y. (2014). "The co-occurrence of autism and attention deficit hyperactivity disorder in children - what do we know?" *Frontiers in Human Neuroscience*, 8, 268. https://doi.org/10.3389/fnhum.2014.00268

Loughborough University. (2023, July 31). "Nursery children happily ate vegetables 60% of the time when offered them at breakfast – new study." (VIDEO). https://www.lboro.ac.uk/schools/sport-exercise-health-sciences/news/2023/nursery-children-happily-eat-vegetables/#:~:text=%E2%80%9CIt's%20thought%20to%20be%20an,those%20flavours%20and%20those%20tastes.

Rattan, A., Savani, K., Chugh, D., & Dweck, C. S. (2015). "Leveraging mindsets to promote academic achievement." *Perspectives on Psychological Science*, 10(6), 721–726. https://doi.org/10.1177/1745691615599383

Cotruș, A., Stanciu, C., & Bulborea, A. A. (2012). "EQ vs. IQ Which is Most Important in the Success or Failure of a Student?" *Procedia: Social &*

Behavioral Sciences, 46, 5211–5213. https://doi.org/10.1016/j.sbspro.2012.06.411

Brown, T. E. (2014). "Smart But Stuck: Emotions in Teens and Adults with ADHD. Wiley.
Goleman, D. (1995). Emotional Intelligence: Why It Can Matter More Than IQ. Bantam Books.

Kristensen, H. A., Parker, J. D. A., Taylor, R. N., Keefer, K. V., Kloosterman, P. H., & Summerfeldt, L. J. (2014). "The relationship between trait emotional intelligence and ADHD symptoms in adolescents and young adults." *Personality and Individual Differences*, 65, 36–41. https://doi.org/10.1016/j.paid.2014.01.031

Langberg, J. M., Arnold, L. E., Flowers, A. M., Altaye, M., Epstein, J. N., & Molina, B. S. (2010). "Assessing Homework Problems in Children with ADHD: Validation of a Parent-Report Measure and Evaluation of Homework Performance Patterns." *School Mental Health*, 2(1), 3–12. https://doi.org/10.1007/s12310-009-9021-x

Thomas, N., & Karuppali, S. (2022). "The efficacy of visual activity schedule intervention in reducing problem behaviors in children with Attention-Deficit/Hyperactivity Disorder between the age of 5 and 12 years: a Systematic review." Soa. Ceongso'nyeon Jeongsin Yihag, 33(1), 2–15. https://doi.org/10.5765/jkacap.210021

FacelessOldWoman1234. (2021). *I love my kid, but I am so exhausted by his ADHD* [Online forum post]. Reddit. https://www.reddit.com/r/ADHD/comments/l9ykbs/i_love_my_kid_but_i_am_so_exhausted_by_his_adhd/

Ok-Veterinarian-5606. (2024). *Feel like I am drowning raising my ADHD son* [Online forum post]. Reddit.

https://www.reddit.com/r/Parenting/comments/1be9eul/feel_like_i_am_drowning_raising_my_adhd_son/

Chronis, A. M., Chacko, A., Fabiano, G. A., Wymbs, B. T., & Pelham, W. E., Jr (2004). "Enhancements to the behavioral parent training paradigm for families of children with ADHD: review and future directions." *Clinical Child and Family Psychology Review*, 7(1), 1–27. https://doi.org/10.1023/b:ccfp.0000020190.60808.a4

Mikami, A. Y., & Pfiffner, L. J. (2008). "Sibling relationships among children with ADHD. Journal of attention disorders." 11(4), 482–492. https://doi.org/10.1177/1087054706295670

Lorenc, E. S., Mallett, R., & Lewis-Peacock, J. A. (2021). "Distraction in Visual Working Memory: Resistance is Not Futile." *Trends in Cognitive Sciences,* 25(3), 228–239. https://doi.org/10.1016/j.tics.2020.12.004

Maier, S. F., & Seligman, M. E. (2016). "Learned helplessness at fifty: Insights from neuroscience." *Psychological Review*, 123(4), 349–367. https://doi.org/10.1037/rev0000033

Leonard, J. (2023, May 23). "What is learned helplnessness?" Medical News Today. https://www.medicalnewstoday.com/articles/325355#history

National Heart, Lung, and Blood Institute. (2022, March 24). "Why Is Sleep Important?" https://www.nhlbi.nih.gov/health/sleep/why-sleep-important#:~:text=During%20sleep%2C%20your%20body%20is,long%2Dterm)%20health%20problems.

Newmark, S. (2021, May 1). "Can Magnesium Help ADHD Symptoms?" ADDitude. https://www.additudemag.com/can-magnesium-help-adhd-symptoms/

Pacheco, D., & Rosen, D. (2024, March 7). "Best Temperature for Sleep." Sleep Foundation. https://www.sleepfoundation.org/bedroom-environment/best-temperature-for-sleep

Tamana, S. K., Ezeugwu, V., Chikuma, J., Lefebvre, D. L., Azad, M. B., Moraes, T. J., Subbarao, P., Becker, A. B., Turvey, S. E., Sears, M. R., Dick, B. D., Carson, V., Rasmussen, C., CHILD study Investigators, Pei, J., & Mandhane, P. J. (2019). "Screen-time is associated with inattention problems in preschoolers: Results from the CHILD birth cohort study." PloS one, 14(4), e0213995. https://doi.org/10.1371/journal.pone.0213995

Furman, W., & Buhrmester, D. (1992). "Age and sex differences in perceptions of networks of personal relationships." *Child Development*, 63(1), 103–115. https://doi.org/10.1111/j.1467-8624.1992.tb03599.x

Telzer, E. H., Fuligni, A. J., Lieberman, M. D., Miernicki, M. E., & Galván, A. (2015). "The quality of adolescents' peer relationships modulates neural sensitivity to risk taking." *Social Cognitive and Affective Neuroscience*, 10(3), 389–398. https://doi.org/10.1093/scan/nsu064

Doucleff, M. (2021). *Hunt, Gather, Parent: What Ancient Cultures Can Teach Us about Raising Children.* HarperCollins Publishers.

Printed in Great Britain
by Amazon